The

Caterer and Hotelkeeper
Guide to the Internet

The
Caterer and Hotelkeeper
Guide to the Internet

David Grant and Peter McBride

BUTTERWORTH
HEINEMANN

OXFORD AUCKLAND BOSTON JOHANNESBURG MELBOURNE NEW DELHI

Butterworth-Heinemann
Linacre House, Jordan Hill, Oxford OX2 8DP
225 Wildwood Avenue, Woburn, MA 01801-2041
A division of Reed Educational and Professional Publishing Ltd

Ⓡ A member of the Reed Elsevier plc group

First published 2000

TRADEMARKS/REGISTERED TRADEMARKS
Computer hardware and software brand names mentioned in this book are
protected by their respective trademarks and are acknowledged.

British Library Cataloguing in Publication Data
A catalogue record for this book is available from the British Library

ISBN 0 7506 4896 1

Designed and typeset by P.K. McBride, Southampton

Printed and bound in Great Britain

Contents

Part 1:

About the Internet

▼
▼
▼
▼
▼
▼
▼
▼
▼
▼

Foreword

At the end of 1999, American dictionary *Websters* declared its word of the 20th century: the one that was more important and significant than any other in the life of the last 100 years. What was that word?

Internet.

In 1999 more than 50 million people used the Internet to research their travel plans, a staggering rise of 1500% since 1996. This shows just how important a presence on the web is to any hospitality business, but there are many who understandably find the whole thing too daunting to contemplate.

Relax, help is at hand. This guide will answer enough questions to make even the most hardened technophobe realise that the Internet is there to work for them, not against them – just give it a chance.

Andrew Davies, Technology Editor, *Caterer and Hotelkeeper*

Preface

This book has been written for people working in the hotel and catering industry. It aims to be a practical introduction to the Internet, showing how you can make it work for you in your business.

The first part of this book is primarily designed for those readers with little or no knowledge of the Internet. It introduces the main ideas, the essential software and the key skills. However, we would hope that more experienced Internet users will find it useful to read the material on Net directories, search engines and e-mail. A good understanding of these is essential if you want to make the best use of the Internet.

In Part 2, we turn the focus on using the Internet in your business, looking at why you should use it, and how you can use it most effectively. We are not trying to turn you into Web designers – there isn't space in a book this size to cover even half of the skills and knowledge that you need to be able to create and maintain your own site. Our aim is to give you enough understanding of the concepts and the processes so that you can make sensible decisions about taking your business on-line. If you are inspired you to get stuck in and create your own site, you may find *HTML Made Simple* and *FrontPage Made Simple* useful.

The Internet changes constantly, so please accept that what you read in these pages was correct when we wrote it, but is not necessarily correct now! The *Caterer and Hotelkeeper* magazine has a regular Web Watch feature that covers developements on the Internet, with special reference to the trade, but if you really want to keep up with the Net, get on-line!

David Grant and Peter McBride

June 2000

What is the Internet anyway?

▼
▼
▼
▼
▼

The Net and the Web ◀

E-mail ◀

Newsgroups and mailing lists ◀

FTP ◀

How big!?!?!?!? ◀

Names and addresses ◀

URLs ◀

The Net and the Web

Let's clear up a common confusion before we start – the Internet and the World Wide Web are not one and the same! The *Internet* is the hardware – the computers and all the links between them – and the software that allows them to communicate with each other. The *World Wide Web* is a means of publishing information over the Internet, and has become its most popular use – hence the common confusion.

The Internet

> Network – a set of linked computers. On a local area network (LAN), users can share printers and other resources. On any network, including the Internet, users can communicate and share data.

The Internet is a set of *inter*linked *net*works. It started 30 years ago linking just four small networks, owned by the US military, but has grown enormously since then. Nowadays it links millions of networks, large and small, government and private, commercial and academic, throughout the world. Some of these networks act as *Internet Service Providers*, offering a route by which members of the public and/or businesses can get into the Internet.

> Internet Service Provider (ISP) – a firm that gives the public access to the internet through the phone lines. Also called Access Providers.

The interlinked nature of the connections is crucial. When any computer on the Net tries to contact any other, there are always several alternative paths that it can take. This makes the Internet very robust – if a link gets broken, the connection will be quickly remade through another route. And, as you will see later, you can make this work for you – if data seems to be coming in slowly, it sometimes pays to break the connection and try again, as next time you may get a faster link.

The linked computers vary from giant supercomputers through desktop PCs, down to little handhelds. They are owned and run by thousands of separate universities, government agencies, businesses and individuals.

The information here may be out of date. Anything you read about the Internet may be out of date! It changes so fast that by the time anything gets printed, it may have been overtaken by events. If you want to know what's happening NOW get onto the Net and watch the changes from the inside.

Some of these computers – known as *hosts* – provide services to the Internet. They publish information, store files, link to cameras or other devices, or carry out crucial 'backroom' jobs, monitoring and maintaining the links in the Net and passing data between them. Most of the computers that use the Internet only link up to it from time to time. They are the ones owned by the ordinary users – you and me – who connect by dialling in through the normal telephone lies, as and when we need to access its services.

The Internet is a tribute to what can be done with a little common sense and cooperation. It spans the world, providing information and services to tens of millions of people simultaneously, transporting unimaginable quantities of data swiftly and efficiently, There is no central governing body, though there is an Internet Society, which coordinates and standardises the methods used. The Internet relies on cooperation, driven by goodwill and enlightened self-interest. And it works!

Browsing the Web – the hand shows we've found a hyperlink (see p. 4)

▼
▼

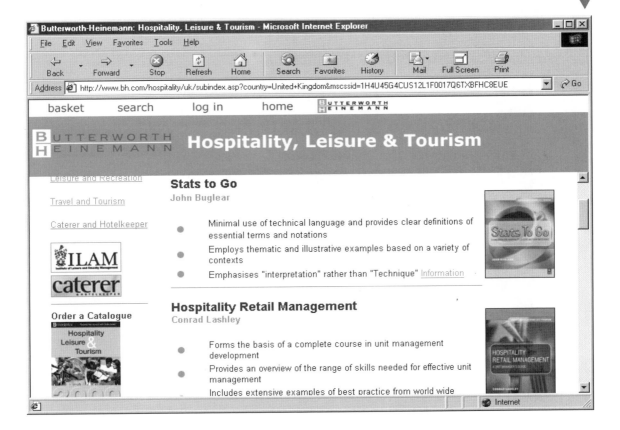

The World Wide Web

Hyperlink – text or a graphic that, when clicked with a mouse, takes you to another part of the Web page or to a page elsewhere on the Web. Text links are usually blue and underlined.

This is the most active and fastest-growing aspect of the Internet. It consists of countless pages, held in millions of computers across the world, accessed and viewed through a Web browser and all joined together by *hyperlinks*. These give simple one-click connections from an image or some text to another page, elsewhere within the same computer or on another computer somewhere – anywhere – on the Web.

The Web is viewed through a browser, such as IE, seen here at Horsebridge Station restaurant ▼ ▼

Most pages are illustrated with still or animated graphics, though some use simpler – but faster – text-only displays. Some have video or sound clips that you can enjoy on-line; others have links to files – programs, documents, pictures or multimedia clips – that you can download onto your computer. Some pages work interactively with the reader, or act as places where users can meet and chat – by typing or by talking.

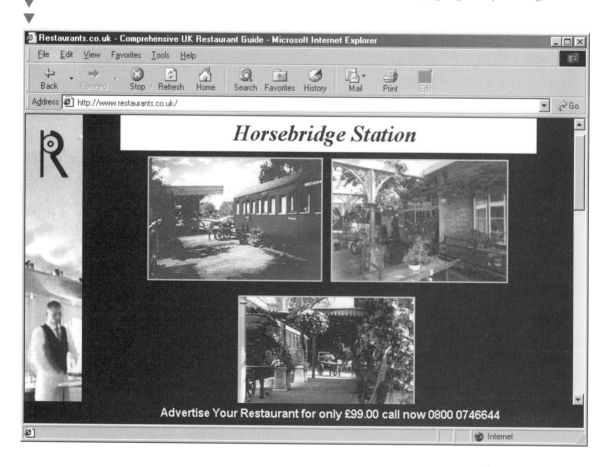

The Web is vast and fairly disorganised, but nevertheless, it's not too difficult to find things. Net directories and search engines (Chapter 3) have organised sets of links to pages, and many pages will have links to others on related topics.

Anyone can publish their own pages on the Web – and it's easy. The tricky bits are getting people to come to them, and to stay and read them! The second half of this book aims to show you how to do these.

E-mail

Though less glamourous than the Web, e-mail ('e' for electronic) is arguably more useful. E-mail allows you to communicate and exchange files quickly and cheaply with other Internet users. You can send a message half way round the world in a matter of minutes, and all it costs is a few seconds of telephone time. In developing this book, the authors used e-mail not only to exchange ideas, but also to send text files, images

Communications between the authors were mainly by e-mail

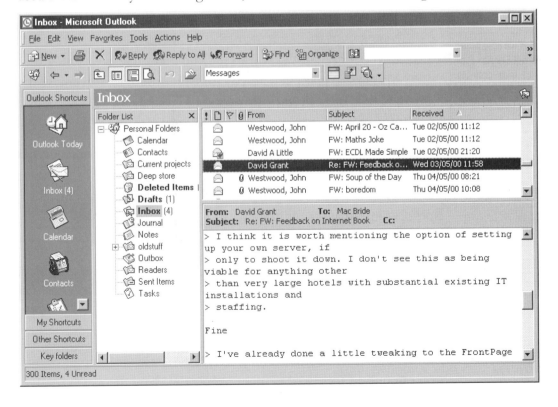

E-mail gives you a simple means of communicating with potential clients

and typeset pages backwards and forwards for checking and correcting – it's quicker, cheaper and more reliable than the post!

E-mail gives you a fast and simple means of communicating with potential clients. They can contact you by e-mail from your Web page, and you can respond quickly, sending details or confirming a booking.

Newsgroups and mailing lists

They are a combination of bulletin boards and newsletters, with each dedicated to a specific interest, topic, hobby, profession or obsession. At the last count, there were over 30,000 different newsgroups, plus a smaller set of mailing lists.

Mailing lists and news groups are organised in slightly different ways.

▷ A mailing list is a direct extension of e-mail. Messages to the list are sent individually to all the people whose names are on it. You have to join the list to get the messages.

▷ Newsgroups are more centralised. The messages – here called articles – are initially sent to the computer that hosts the group. *News servers* collect new articles from the groups several times a day and hold them in store. If you want to read the news, you connect to your news server and download articles from there.

> News server – a computer at an Internet Service Provider's site that collects and stores news-group articles for the benefit of its users.

Neither newsgroups nor mailing lists are of much value in marketing, but they can be very valuable for sharing ideas with others in the same business, for discussing common problems and for tracking down specialist information and resources.

FTP

FTP stands for File Transfer Protocol and is the standard method for copying files across the Internet. FTP hosts hold archives that anyone can search and download files from. Some hosts have directories into which you can upload files, so that other people can share them.

The sort of things that you might want to download include tools to help you create Web pages – and there are lots available, at little or no cost.

You can download files through a Web browser, but to upload you normally need a dedicated FTP program such as WS_FTP (find out more at http://www.ipswitch.com). You may also need this to upload your pages when you set up your own Web site.

> Download – copy a file from a site on the Internet onto your computer.
>
> Upload – copy a file from your computer to a site on the Internet.

How big!?!?!?!?

Because there are so many different organisations involved, with no single body controlling the Internet, and because it is constantly growing, no one knows for sure how big the Internet really is. The figures that follow are based on sampling, trends and earlier counts.

In 1989 there were around 100,000 host computers connected to the Internet. It reached 500,000 by mid-1991 and has been doubling every year since. At the time of writing (mid-2000) the total is over 75 million – and these are just the *host* computers, the ones that provide services to the Internet.

> Host computer – one that provides a service for Internet users. The service may be pages of information, access to files for downloading, a place to meet and chat with other users, or a complex interactive service.

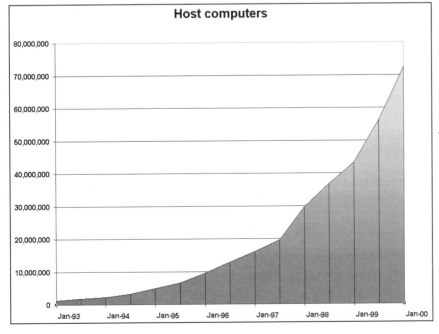

The Internet grows at an amazing rate – these are just the host computers . Source: Internet Software Consortium (http://www.isc.org/)

There has been an exponential growth in the number of domains – named sites (see page 10). These increased steadily to 70,000 by 1995, leapt to 1 million by 1997 and will have passed 100 million by the time you read this. The bare statistics may be a little misleading – at first, only large organisations had domain names; now, many individuals and small businesses also have their own domain names.

Look at the number of people with Internet access, and you will see the same rapid growth. Back in 1995, there were an estimated 35 million people on-line, worldwide. Only five years later, the best guess is nearly 300 million! The take-up varies dramatically in different countries. In the USA, where the Internet started and where it grew first and fastest, around half the population is on-line; after a slightly slower start, the UK has reached almost the same level; in France and Germany, about 20% are on-line; in China, its less than 2% – though that is still 15 million people!

Until quite recently, English was far and away the language most commonly used on the Internet – largely because the vast majority of

Mother-tongues of Internet users. Source: Global Reach (http://www.glreach.com)

▼
▼

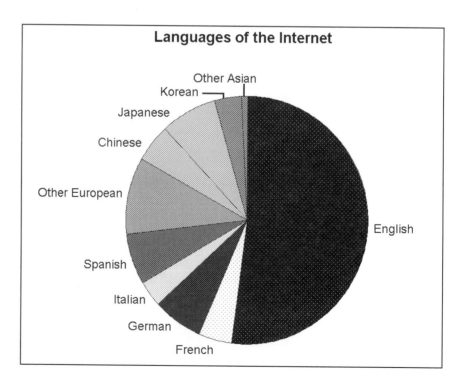

organisations providing online services and information were based in North America and the UK. Though an increasing amount of information on the Web is in other languages, but English is still dominant. This has obvious advantages for any English speaker who wants to sell their product through the Web.

Names and addresses

With something as big as the Internet, you need a well-organised naming system to find your way around. Every host computer and net-work has its own unique *domain name* – it also has a number, but you will very rarely need to know these. Computers and smaller networks within larger ones may also have their own names, and every user has an address.

A domain name has have several parts, separated by dots. The first part is usually derived directly from the name of the organisation, and perhaps a section within it. The next part is determined by the nature of the organisation. At the end is a country code, except where the organisation is international or based in the USA.

Commonly-found nature and country codes include:

com commercial (US and international)
co commercial (within a country elsewhere)
edu educational (US)
ac educational (elsewhere)
net network provider
org non-commercial organisation
gov government
uk United Kingdom
au Australia
fr France
de Germany
es Spain
jp Japan

With something as big as the Internet, you need a well-organised naming system to find your way around

Domain name – the part of an Internet address that identifies a computer or a network.

Some examples of domain names:

vnet.ibm.com

The **vnet** network within **IBM**, a **com**mercial organisation.

repp.co.uk

Reed **E**ducational and **P**rofessional **P**ublishing, a **com**mercial organisation based in the **UK**.

gn.apc.org

Green**N**et, a member of the **A**ssociation for **P**rogressive **C**ommunications **org**anisation.

oregon.uoregon.edu

The main **Oregon** site in the University of **Oregon** (USA).

We'll come back to domain names – and how you can get your own – in Chapter 6.

URLs

Every page on the World Wide Web and every file on the Internet has its own URL – Uniform Resource Locator – which tells you what kind of thing it is, what it is called and where to find it. For example, the URL of David's own hotel site is:

http://www.corisande.com

And Mac's home page can be found at:

http://homepages.tcp.co.uk/~macbride

The first part of the URL defines the nature of the address. The main types are:

http:	World Wide Web page
ftp:	file in an FTP archive
news:	newsgroup
mailto:	e-mail address

The rest of the URL identifies the page, file or person, and tells you where to find it.

For most of us, the only URLs that we are likely to use are those of Web pages and e-mail addresses.

Web pages normally – but by no means always – start **www** and are followed by the domain name. This gives you the Web site name, and is enough to reach the top level or 'index' page for the site. You will often see site addresses written with a slash at the end. This simply marks it as the top level page, and can be omitted. Thus:

> **http://www.corisande.com**

> **http://www.corisande.com/**

will both take you to the front door of David's hotel.

The site URL may be followed by the names of folders – and sometimes folders within folders – and of specific pages; e.g.

> **http://homepages.tcp.co.uk/~macbride/msbooks.htm**

This will find the Made Simple books page in my folder at my ISP.

We will leave e-mail addresses until we look at e-mail in Chapter 4.

The key points to note about URLs are these:

▷ You have to get an URL exactly right if you want to reach the Web page or the e-mail recipient. Near enough is not good enough!

▷ You will rarely need to type in URLs and very rarely need to type them twice. Web browsers and e-mail software have simple but efficient systems for capturing, saving and reusing URLs.

2

Setting up your system

▼
▼
▼
▼
▼

Hardware ◀

Internet Service Providers ◀

Software ◀

Logging on ◀

Internet Explorer ◀

General options ◀

Security ◀

Netscape Navigator ◀

To get on-line, you need:

▷　　**Hardware** – a computer, modem and telephone line;

▷　　**Software** – for surfing the Web, downloading files and handling the mail and news.

▷　　**An Internet Service Provider (ISP)** – to connect you to the Net.

Hardware

The computer

You do not need a high-speed, high-capacity machine to access the Internet

You do not need a high-speed, high-capacity machine to access the Internet. Most Web pages and e-mail consist of simple text and still images. Any PC built within the last five or six years is perfectly capable of handling 95+% of anything you'll meet on-line.

If you are buying a new computer, all Apple Macs and 'Internet-ready' PCs come with integral modems and all the software that you need to get started – you can pick up other software off the Net as you want it.

The modem

Modem – a device that converts digital signals from a computer into analogue ones for transmission over the phone lines (and vice versa).

Bit – (Binary digit) the number 1 or 0, represented electronically as *on or off*.

Byte – the smallest unit of data, composed of 8 bits. A byte can hold a character or a number between 0 and 256.

If you want to use an existing, older, computer and it does not have a modem in it, or attached to it, you will need to buy and fit one – don't worry, modems are cheap and easy to install!

The quality of the modem dictates the *maximum* speed at which it can transfer data. Speed is measured in Baud – bits per second. There are 8 bits to a byte, but all data transmissions have extra addressing and error-checking information attached to them, so divide by 10 to get the approximate *bytes* per second speed, or by 10,000 to get the Kilobyte rate.

At the time of writing, 56.6K modems are the norm, and cost around £50. These can move data at 56,600 Baud, or 5.6Kb per second – that's around 1Mb in 3 minutes. In theory, these speeds can double with special compression techniques, but in practice, data is rarely transferred at anything like that rate. E-mail isn't too bad, typically transferring at 3 to

4Kb per second, but the Web can be very slow. The files that make up Web pages normally come in at around 2Kb per second, but this can drop to below 500 bytes per second. It's simply a matter of traffic. At busy times, there may be millions of people trying to use the main connections through the Internet, and all of the more popular sites are likely to have tens of thousands of vistors all trying to get in at the same time. A fast modem won't cure the traffic jams – it will just make sure that there are no hold-ups at your end.

the Web can be
very slow

Ports

All computers have one or more *serial ports* for getting data into and out of the machine. On a PC there are four, called COM1, COM2, COM3 and COM4. (COM is short for COMunications.)

> Port – connection between the PC and other hardware. Normally a socket on the back of the PC, but expansion slots can also be ports.

A port may be a socket at the back of the PC's case, or reached through an expansion slot inside. Plugging a card modem into any slot will give it access to the port, though you may have to tell it which one.

▷ Most PCs have a serial port at the back of the machine. This is COM1, and may have a mouse plugged into it.

▷ Some PCs have two external serial ports, COM1 and COM2.

An external modem must be allocated the port number that it is plugged into; a card modem can be allocated any available internal port.

Newer PCs have one or more USB ports. These can be used for connecting peripherals such as scanners, printers – and modems. Serial and USB-connected modems give the same performance, so it doesn't matter which you buy – just make sure that it is plugged into the right port!

> USB (Universal Serial Bus) – a new method of connecting peripherals, giving faster data transfer. There's no speed gain with a modem, as the pace is set by the phone line, which is even slower.

Buying a modem

▷ Internal modems are easy to install and leave the serial port free.

▷ With an external modem, you must have a free serial/USB port.

▷ If you are connecting to the normal public telephone lines, you can only legally use BABT approved modems in the UK.

▷ Most modems now are fax modems, which you can also use to send and receive faxes from your PC.

Modem settings

With the modem, as with much else in Windows 98, you can generally leave it to the system to find the best settings for it. There are, however, a couple of things that you might want to set to suit yourself. These relate to how you use the phone and the modem.

1 Open the Control Panel and double-click 📞 Modems.

2 Click the Properties button.

3 Switch to Connection panel.

4 If other people use the line, tick Wait for dial tone. This will stop the modem from trying to dial out while someone else is on the phone.

5 Set the Disconnect if idle time to 10 minutes – this is not as long as it sounds. The modem is 'idle' when you are reading a Web page or e-mail.

6 Click OK and close the Modem dialog box.

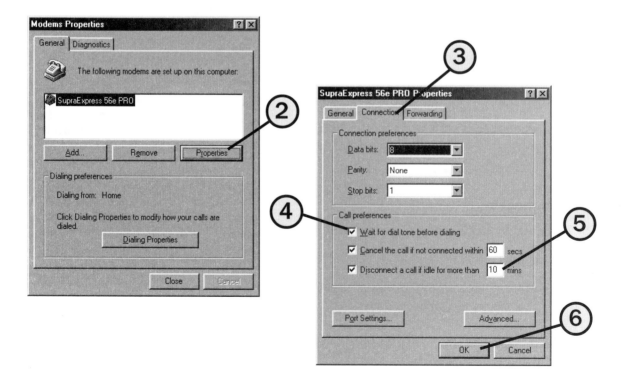

Phone connection

You connect to your Internet Service Provider through the normal phone lines. The only extra kit you may need is an extension kit and wall-mounted socket to put a socket within reach of your desktop.

ISP (Internet Service Provider) – a firm that gives the public access to the Internet through the phone lines.

Internet Service Providers

If you are going to put your business on the Web, then you will normally get access to the Internet through whoever hosts your Web space, so leave a decision on which provider until you've tackled that question. In the meantime, if you do not already have Internet access, you really should get a temporary connection so that you can get online and explore.

You will normally get access to the Internet through whoever hosts your Web space

▷ Sign up with BT Click (see page 19), Freeserve or one of the other free access services – though not one that ties you into changing your phone line or other long-term commitment. All it will cost you is call charges when you are online – about a penny a minute.

▷ Take advantage of a free trial offer with AOL. They currently offer 10 hours totally free – no phone charges – online try-out time. But watch out, they will start to collect fees from your credit card as soon as the time runs out, and it can take a while to get through to them by phone to cancel the subscription at the end of the trial.

Software

There are two aspects to configuring a new connection – the network software within your PC, and the connection to the service provider.

Dial-Up Networking

Click the **Start** button, point to **Programs**, then **Accessories**, then **Communications**. You should find **Dial-up Networking** on that submenu. If it is not there, now is the time to install it – it will only take a couple of minutes.

Dial-Up Networking – the Windows software that handles connections to the Internet through the phone lines.

1 Open the Control Panel and double-click on the Network icon.

2 Click Add.

3 For the type of component, select Protocol and click Add.

4 Select Microsoft in the Manufacturers list and TCP/IP as the Protocol.

5 Click OK to close the Protocol dialog box.

6 Click OK at the Network dialog box.

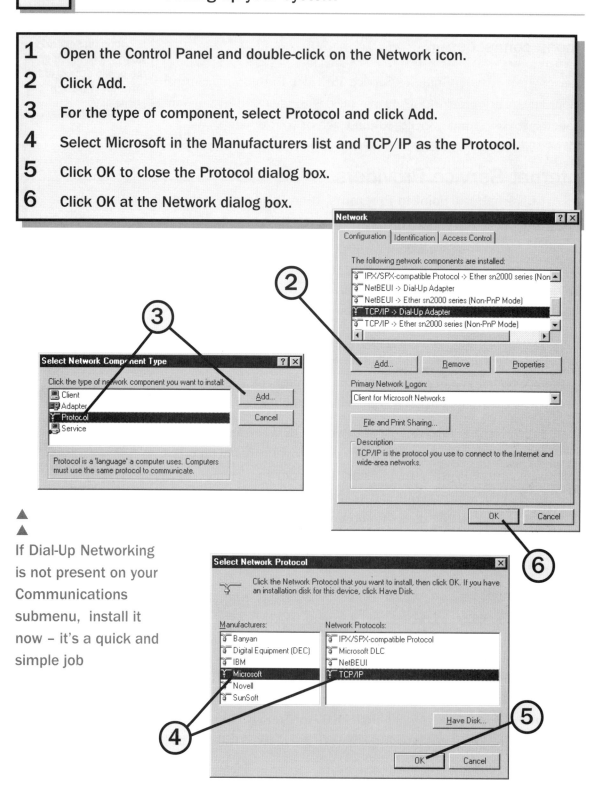

▲
▲

If Dial-Up Networking is not present on your Communications submenu, install it now – it's a quick and simple job

Making a connection

Once the Network software is in place, you can set up the connection. Here's how to connect to BT Click – a no-subscription, penny-a-minute service. You might like to use this while you have a look around the Internet to see what services are on offer and decide which access provider you would like to sign up with.

1 Click **Start**, point to Programs, then Accessories, then Communications and select Dial-Up Networking.

2 Click Make New Connection.

3 In the Wizard enter a name to idenitify the connection then click Next.

4 Enter the phone number – the Area and Country code must also be given unless it is a local number.

5 Click Next, and Finish at the summary screen which follows.

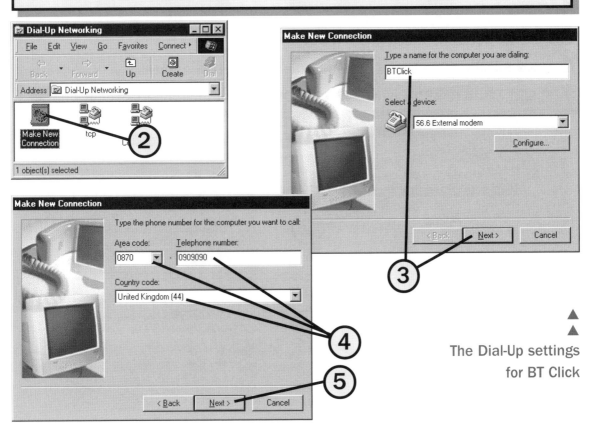

The Dial-Up settings for BT Click

Setting Properties

The New Connection wizard tells the computer how to reach to the ISP. To tell it how to behave when it gets there, you have to set the Properties. These determine how data is transmitted between you and the ISP, and which addresses to use. Some ISPs give you a fixed IP (Internet Protocol) address, others have their server allocate an address when you log on. The ISP may have one or two DNS (Domain Name Server) addresses.

> DNS address – the Internet address of the ISP's computer that will link you to the Internet.

Here are the settings for BT Click. Ask your ISP what settings are needed. You may not need to do anything as some providers have self-installing software which will do all this for you!

1 Right-click on the new connection and select Properties.

2 On the Server Types tab, select *PPP:Internet...* for the Type.

3 Check *Enable software compression* and *TCP/IP* – clearing all others.

4 Click TCP/IP Settings.

5 Select Server assigned IP address.

6 Set Specify name server and enter the Primary DNS address.

7 Click OK to close the panel and click OK again at the Properties dialog box.

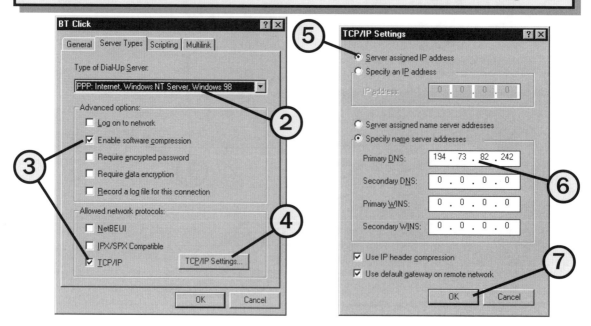

Both the IP and DNS addresses will be in their raw form – four sets of numbers, between 0 and 255, separated by dots. See page 85 for more on number addresses.

Logging on

Log on – connect to an
on-line service.

OK, so you have got your user name and password – either by signing up online or over the phone – and have set up the Dial-Up Networking connection. It's now time to plug in the phone line, turn on the modem and try to log on to your service.

These next steps just connect you to the Internet. To do anything useful, you must also run your browser or your e-mail software. You can do this before or after you log on.

1   Click (or double-click) the connection's icon.

2   Enter your User name (only needed the first time) and Password.

3   Turn on the Save Password option – if you are the only one who has access to the computer.

4   Click Connect.

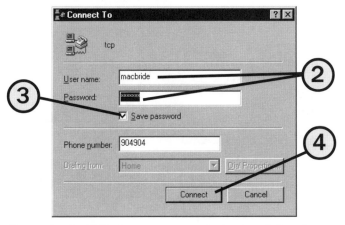

Turn **Save Password** off if the computer is in a public place. You will then have to enter your password every time you log on, but it will prevent other people from using your connection

Setting up your system

▼
▼
▼
▼
▼

To view and travel through the Web you need a browser

Internet Explorer

To view and travel through the World Wide Web you need a browser, and Internet Explorer 5 (IE5) is the browser supplied with the Windows 98 package. Let's have a look at it.

The main part of the window is used for the display of Web pages. On the left is the **Explorer Bar**, which can be opened to give simpler navigation when searching the Internet, or using the Favorites (page 48) or History (page 47). Above this are the control elements. The **Menu bar** has the full command set, with the most commonly used ones duplicated in the **Standard Toolbar**. There are also toolbars for **Links** (quick links to selected places) and **Radio** (for using Web radio).

Title of current page   Menu bar   Standard Toolbar

Address

Explorer Bar

Open folder

Status bar

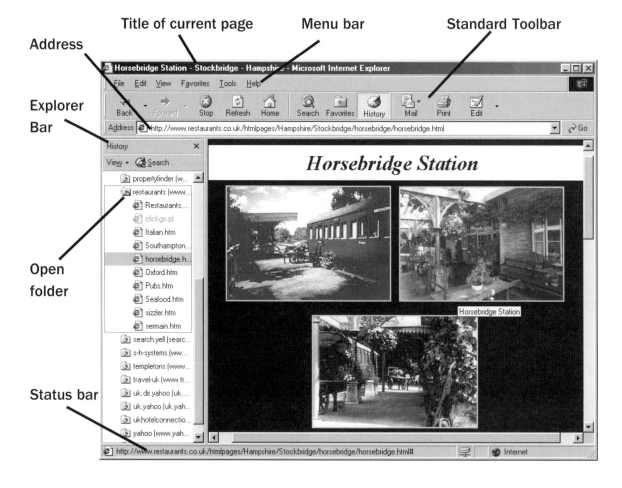

The **Address** shows you where you are. You can type an URL here to open a page. Typed URLs are stored. When you next want to revisit the site you can drop down the list and selected the URL from there, or start to type it and IE5 will complete it for you.

The **Status Bar** shows the address behind hyperlinks, and the progress of incoming files.

View options

You can adjust the display with the options on the **View** menu.

▷   Turn the **Status Bar** and the **Toolbars** on or off.

▷   Open or close the **Explorer Bar**.

▷   Use **Customize…** to change the layout or selection of icons in the toolbars.

▷   Set the **Text Size** level to make all text and headings larger or smaller.

The Standard Toolbar

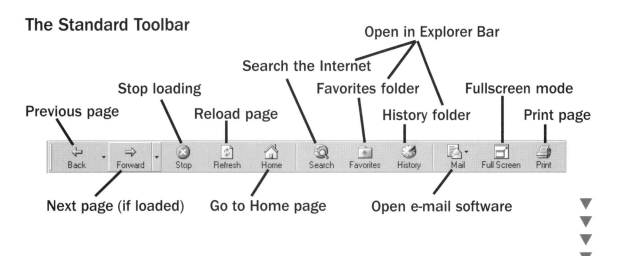

New versions of Internet Explorer are released regularly and available free from Microsoft. Go to **www.microsoft.com** if you want the latest version.

General options

The Internet Options control many aspects of Explorer's display and of how it works. Most of these can be left at their default settings, though there are a few that will repay early attention. Start on the **General** panel:

> Home page – the page that a browser tries to connect to when it first starts, also used to describe the top page of a Web site.

▷ Choose your **Home page**. This is where IE will go when it starts. Set it to 'blank' or your regular start point (such as a Net directory – see Chapter 3).

▷ When you visit a page, IE stores copies of its files on your hard disk. If you revisit, it will use those copies if the page has not changed, saving download time. The **Settings** determine how much space is allocated to storage and the **History** settings control how long the copies are retained. The defaults are quite sensible – leave them until you have been surfing a while.

▷ Web page designers can set the **Colors** and **Fonts** on a page, but often do not bother, leaving them at their defaults. You can set you own defaults, and if you need maximum visibility, you can insist that these are always used via the **Accessibility** options.

1   Open the Tools menu and select Internet Options...

2   Go to the General panel.

3   For the Home page, type the URL (or click Use Current if you are on that page), or click Use Blank.

4   Click Colors... .

5   To change a colour, click on it then pick a new colour from the palette. Click OK when you have done. Set Fonts in the same way.

6   Click Accessibility... .

7   Set IE to ignore the pages' own colours and fonts – so that yours are used instead.

8   Click OK.

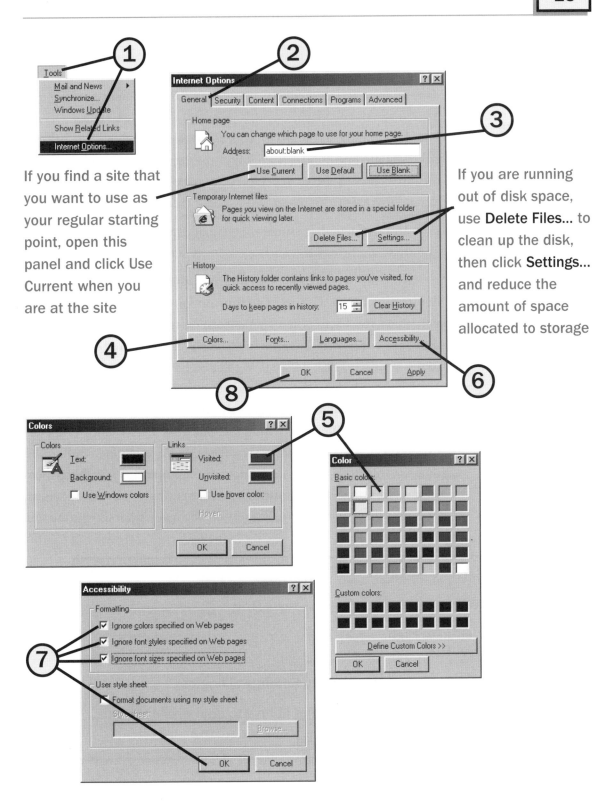

If you find a site that you want to use as your regular starting point, open this panel and click Use Current when you are at the site

If you are running out of disk space, use **Delete Files...** to clean up the disk, then click **Settings...** and reduce the amount of space allocated to storage

Security

Active content should not be able to mess with your hard disks or access your data, but...

Many Web pages have **active content**, i.e. they contain *applets* (small programs) written in Java, ActiveX or other interactive languages. These should not be able to mess with your hard disks or access your data, but hackers sometimes find a way round the restrictions – and anti-virus software is no help here. Active content makes browsing more interesting, and if you stick to major sites, should create no problems.

If you are confident that a site is very safe, add its URL to the Trusted sites list – these are browsed with **Low** security settings

Start with the security of the **Internet zone** (i.e. all Web sites) to **Medium** or **High**. Use the **Custom** option to fine-tune the settings later, when you have more experience. You may, for instance, want to take control of *cookies*. These are small files which are stored on – and read from – your hard disk by some Web sites. Sometimes cookies are very useful, holding your preferences and other user information for sites that you visit regularly and use interactively. Other cookies are of no value to you, but allow the Web site to monitor your visits. Personally, I don't like anyone sticking things on my disk without my permission, but there are some sites that won't let you in without setting cookies, so disabling them is not really viable. The **Prompt** option alerts you to the cookie-setters, but means that you have to OK every cookie if you want to visit the site.

---

1 Go to the Security panel.

2 Pick the Internet zone.

3 Pull the slider up to High.

or

4 Click `Custom Level...` to open the Security Settings dialog box.

5 Scroll down through the display, telling IE how to deal with each type.

6 Click OK to return to the Options panel.

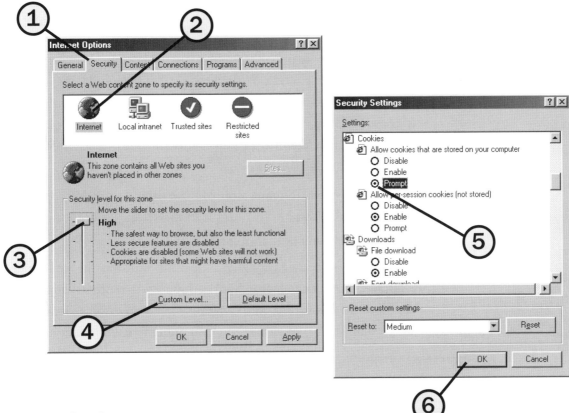

Other Options

If children are going to be using your Internet connection, have a look at the **Content** panel. The settings here allow you to restrict access to sites. There are several ratings services which rate the levels of sex 'n' violence at sites, and you can set what you regard as acceptable levels. Unfortunately there are many totally inoffensive sites that have simply not bothered to submit their pages for a ratings inspection, and are therefore blocked. There are better child-protection systems around, but this is a useful first line of defence and it's free.

If you change your ISP, use the **Connection** panel to set up and to tell IE5 about the new connection.

After you have been surfing for a while, go to the **Advanced** panel and adjust its options to suit the way you work.

▼
▼
▼
▼
▼

The Content settings allow you to restrict access to sites

Netscape Navigator

Internet Explorer is not the only browser! Netscape Navigator is an excellent alternative, and one preferred by many people. Navigator is supplied as part of the comprehensive Communicator suite, which also includes e-mail and newsgroup software, and an HTML editor for creating your own Web pages, plus 'net phone', real-time conferencing and Web chat utilities.

If you want to try Communicator, you can often find it on the CDs on computer magazines, or download it from Netscape's home site at:

http://www.netscape.com

The layout and tools are very similar to those of Internet Explorer

▼
▼

or wherever you see the [N Netscape Now!] button. Be aware that the file is around 10Mb, so will take up to half an hour to download – though that is smaller than the setup files for Internet Explorer. Communicator is easy to install – and to uninstall if you decide that you prefer to use Internet Explorer.

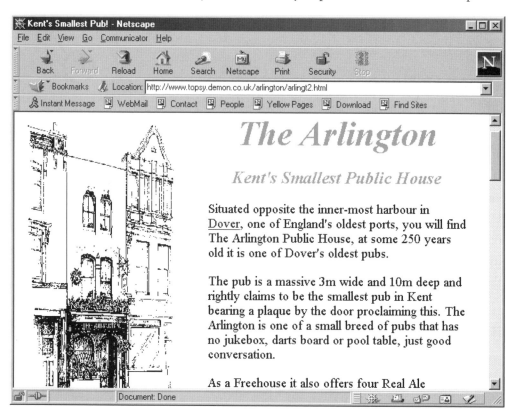

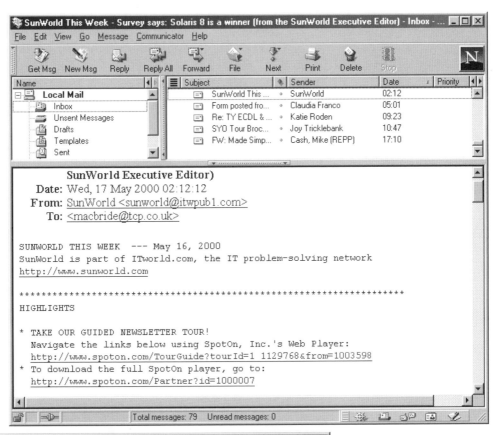

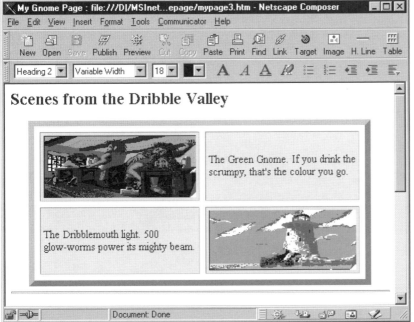

Screenshots from Messenger, the e-mail and news software (above) and Composer, the HTML editor (left). The programs are all well-designed and simple to use

3

Exploring the World Wide Web

▼
▼
▼
▼
▼

Navigating the Web ◀

Using URLs ◀

Net directories ◀

Local Webs ◀

Search engines ◀

The History list ◀

Favorites ◀

Using Netscape Navigator ◀

Navigating the Web

There are essentially three ways to go to places on the Web – all the rest are variations on these:

▷   Follow a hypertext link from one page to another.

▷   Type the address of the page into your browser.

▷   Reuse an address that's stored in your browser.

You have to type or reuse an address to get into the Web, but once there, you will mainly navigate by following links, so let's start with those.

Hypertext links

It's the links that make the Web what it is

You will find hypertext links in their millions in directories and search engines, and in smaller sets on specialist pages run by enthusiasts or organisations, but also scattered liberally throughout the Web. It's the links that make the Web what it is.

A link may take you from one page to another within a site or off to a far-distant site. Some pages will turn out to be treasure troves, full of information or of links to other pages; others – rather more, unfortunately – will be less useful.

Links can be attached to both text and images, and are always easy to spot. When you point at a link, the cursor changes to 🖑 and the Status line shows the address of the linked page.

Links in text are (almost) always underlined and in a different colour from normal text – links are typically blue. The links may be items in a list, or words embedded in other text.

Links in images come in two varieties.

▷   At the simplest, the whole image carries a single link. Typical uses include 'navigation' buttons – with links to the different parts of the site – and thumbnail pictures, which lead to larger versions of themselves. These may – but often do not – have a blue border to show that they are linked.

▷ An image may have any number of links embedded into it, each in its own area. These *image maps* are much favoured by sites that offer regional services or information, as the visitor can simply click on the appropriate area of a geographical map.

> Image map - an image with several hyperlinks, each in its own area. They sometimes really are maps, but any image can be used.

If you are aiming to include a guide to places of interest near your hotel, you might want to investigate image maps – they are not difficult to produce.

If you have gone **Back**, you can use **Forward** to revisit pages in that direction

Use **Back** to return to the page you just came from

An image may be used as a simple button – they are normally easy to spot

Look for the hand

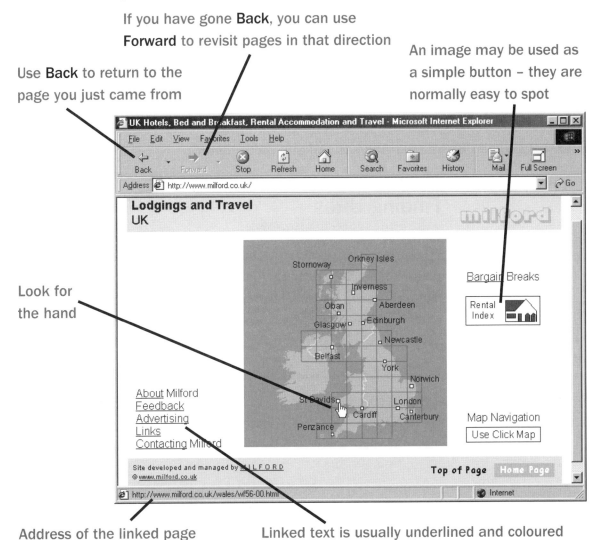

Address of the linked page

Linked text is usually underlined and coloured blue. It may be a separate item or a word or phrase within a larger block of text

Using URLs

All Web browsers have routines for entering URLs. In Internet Explorer they can be typed into the Address slot, or into the Open dialog box that is reached from the File menu.

1   Have the URL to hand – they are not things that you can easily remember accurately!

2   From the File menu select Open.

3   Type in the URL.

4   Click OK.

or

5   Type the URL into the Address slot and press [Enter].

Finding URLs

Of course, before you can use a URL, you must know what it is. So where do you find them? Obviously, the Web is a major source, but you'll find them all over nowadays. They are given in magazines and newspaper articles, on posters, in TV ads and programmes – the URL for the BBC's news service (used opposite) is given at the end of the newscasts.

Once you start exploring the Web, you will find URLs all over the place. Make a note of any interesting ones, or add them to your Favorites (page 48).

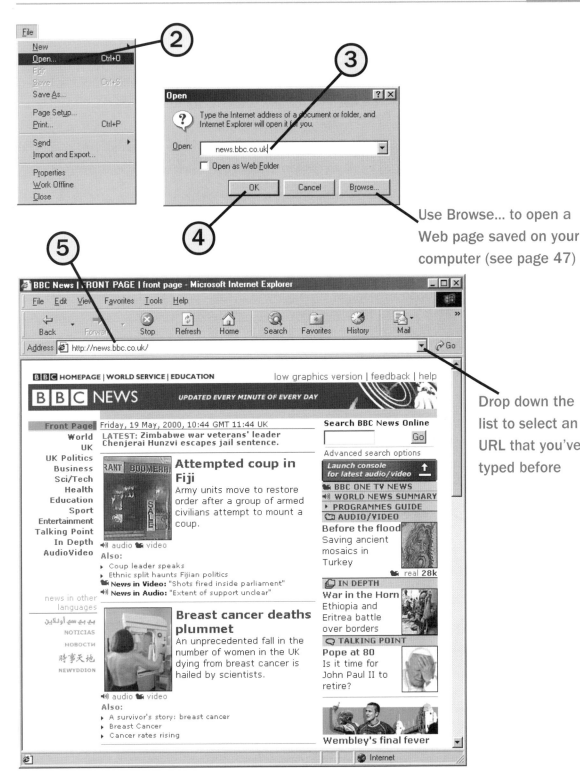

Use Browse... to open a Web page saved on your computer (see page 47)

Drop down the list to select an URL that you've typed before

Net directories

Directories hold links, organised into subjects. In some, all of the linked sites will have been visited and vetted by someone from the directory, so that you have some guarantee of quality and relevance. Others invite people to add links to their own sites. How a directory is compiled matters when you are trying to get your own site noticed (see page 89).

The Web hosts around a dozen large, general-purpose directories, plus many more specialist ones.

Yahoo

Yahoo was one of the first, and is still one of the biggest and best Net directories. It has links to over a million selected Web sites, organised into a hierarchy of categories with extensive cross-referencing. Once you get past the first level, you find a mixture of links to pages and lists of sub-categories, with the links increasing as you go down the hierarchy.

Yahoo! started in the USA. There are now Yahoo!s for many countries – including the UK & Ireland

▼
▼

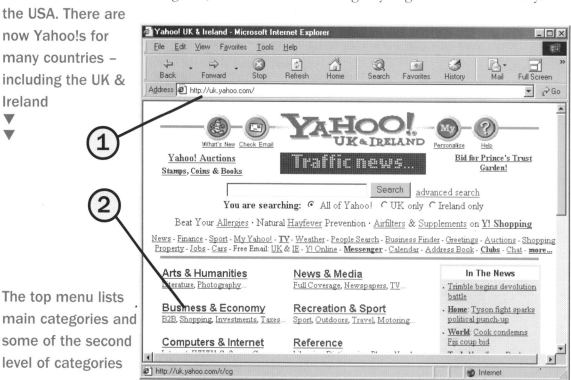

The top menu lists main categories and some of the second level of categories

1 Go to Yahoo at http://uk.yahoo.com *or* www.yahoo.co.uk

2 Click on a category on the main menu.

3 Select a category from the next menu – repeat as necessary.

4 When you reach the links, select one.

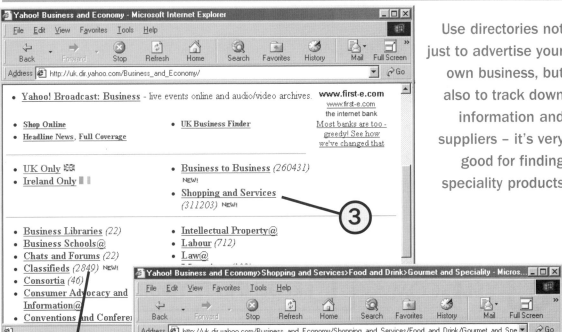

Use directories not just to advertise your own business, but also to track down information and suppliers – it's very good for finding speciality products

The number of links in this sub-category

UK-based directories

If you are searching for UK-based suppliers, or want to bring your Web site (when you've built it!) to a largely UK audience, there are two directories in particular that you should have a look at.

Yell

Yell is the electronic version of Yellow Pages. It has three significant advantages over the paper-based version.

If you have a Web site, it can be linked from your Yell entry ▼ ▼

▷   It gives full coverage of the UK, not just one local area.

▷   There's a map system that gives good directions to the businesses.

▷   If the business has a Web site, it can be linked from here.

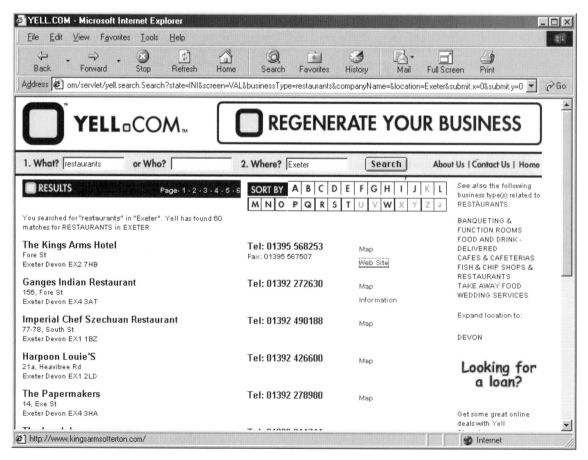

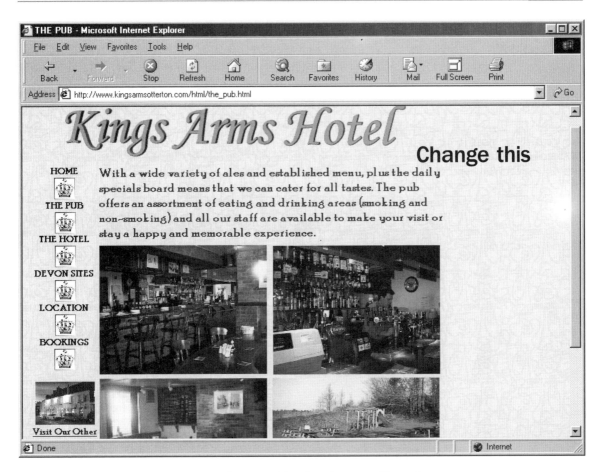

If you are aiming to attract a UK audience, either local or travellers, these three things combine to make Yell a site not to be missed. Searching Yell is very simple – as long as the searcher knows the Yellow Pages category, and 'restaurants', 'hotels' or 'public houses' are all obvious ones – so people can find you easily (and the map will help them to get to you!).

Standard Yell entries are free, and you can sign up on-line or by phone in a matter of minutes. However, if you have a Web site, and want to link that from your Yell entry, there is a charge of £190 p.a. The fee also ensures that your business will be listed at the top of any search results.

If you are looking for suppliers, the fact that you must know the Yellow Pages category can be a real limitation. Where are you going to start looking for haggises for your Burn's Night special? The simplest answer is not in Yell, but in the UK Directory.

▲
▲
A link from Yell can bring people into your establishment

UK Directory

This is not as comprehensive as Yell – which is scarcely surprising as the UK Directory is for business who are on-line, not just on the phone – but it can be a better place to search for suppliers. The directory does organise its entries into categories, but you pick from a menu rather than having to type in the right category name. More importantly – entries have keywords, and you can run simple searches on these.

keyword – word used in a search to identify a directory entry or Web site.

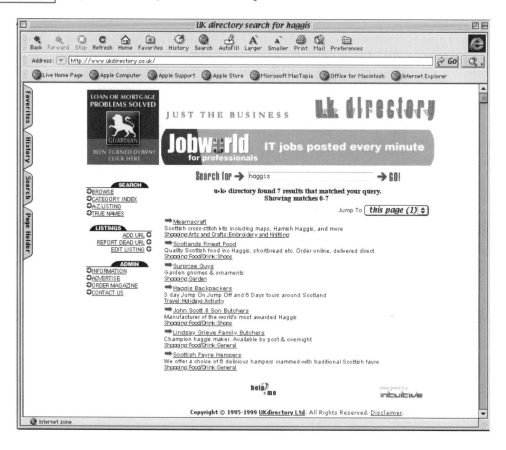

▲
▲
UK Directory is a good place to find suppliers and to market your own business

'Haggis' turned up seven sites, although three of these did not deal in edible haggises – and no cracks please about all haggis being inedible, some of us like them!

When you get round to building your own site, add a link to it at UK Directory. The basic entry into a category, e.g. Entertainment: Eating Out, with a set of keywords is free.

Local Webs

Just because you can reach the whole world through the Web doesn't mean you have to! A local site can provide a good service to a local community, and be a good place to reach a local audience. If your area has such a site, pay it a visit and see if it's the sort of site that you should be using. I would have thought that most restaurants and pubs – and any hotels that catered for functions – that had Web sites should be listed in their local guide.

◀◀ Southampton's local on-line guide, one of a score run by City-Online. Find out more at www.city-online.co.uk

In these guides, listings entries are free,and adverts are very cheap

▼

Search engines

▼
▼
▼
▼
▼

'spider' programs scan the Web, building databases of key words

Search engines have 'spider' or 'crawler' programs that scan the Web constantly, building databases of key words on each site. Engines vary, but the words that are indexed include those designated as 'keywords', plus those used in the title, and sometimes those in the headings and the text of the top page – and possibly lower level pages – of the site.

When you run a search at one of these sites, another program hunts through the database for words that match those you have entered. Again, engines vary, but as a general rule, they will find those pages that contain all or any of the keywords, listing first those that contain all of the words – i.e., those which are the closest matches. They often have advanced search facilities, where you can use logical operators and symbols to define a search more closely. Most of us will never bother with these, as simple searches normally do the trick.

AltaVista

This is one of the most popular search engines – fast, simple to use and with a huge database. A simple search at AltaVista can produce thousands (sometimes millions!) of hits – if this happens, you can try an advanced search to focus on the things that you want.

In this example, and the next at Infoseek, the search is for vegetarian restaurants in Oxford. Here, we simply write in the whole phrase – you could write a proper sentence if you liked, e.g. 'Where can I find out about vegetarian restaurants in Oxford?'

1   Go to AltaVista at: www.altavista.com/

2   Type what you are looking for, e.g. 'vegetarian restaurant Oxford'.

3   Click Search.

4   Click on a link – the first couple of pages will probably have the best hits.

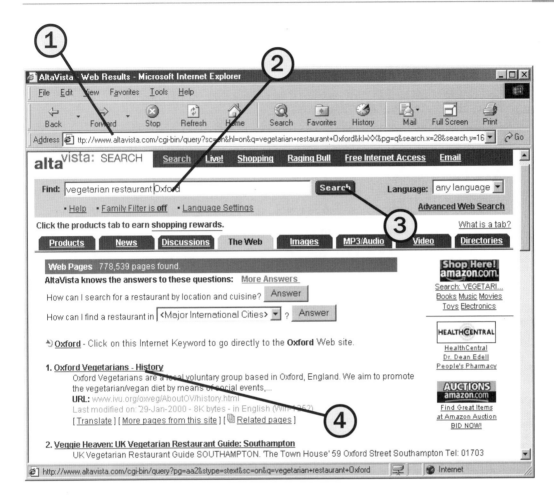

Logical operators

At many search engines you can use these operators to link your search words to give a more closely defined search:

AND   every word must match to produce a hit

OR   any matching word will produce a hit

NOT   ignore pages containing this word

NEAR   linked words must be close together on a page.

The operators can be used singly, or in combination. If they are combined, an AND test is normally done before an OR test, but you can put brackets round an expression to have that tested first.

Running a simple
search at AltaVista

Some examples of logical operators at work:

> vegetarian AND restaurant

will find pages that contain both words.

> vegetarian OR vegan

will find pages that contain either or both words.

> (vegetarian OR vegan) AND restaurant AND Oxford

should find references to non-meat restaurants in Oxford. If the brackets had not been used, this would have found any page containing the word 'vegetarian' – restaurants, recipes, or whatever – and any about vegan restaurants in Oxford.

If you want to see how logical operators can produce better matching sets of results, go to the **Advanced Web seach** page at AltaVista.

---

1   Go to AltaVista at: http://www.altavista.com

2   Click on the Advanced Web search link.

3   Type in your keywords, linking them with the operators AND, OR, NOT and NEAR, using brackets if you want part of the expression to be tested first.

4   Click Search.

Though an advanced search can produce a smaller and better matched set of results than a simple one, they may not be any more useful. With a simple search, AltaVista – like most search engines – lists the results in order of 'relevance', and this is based on how often your search words occur in the page, and whether they are present in the title, headings and designated keywords. The effect is normally to bring the best pages to the top of the results list. With an advanced search, the results are not ranked first, so that the best, closest-matching pages are scattered through the list. (Though note that typing a word into the 'Sort by' box will cause pages containing that word to be listed first.)

The main thing to note here is that there are ways to help bring your Web pages to the top of search results. We will return to this in Chapter 6.

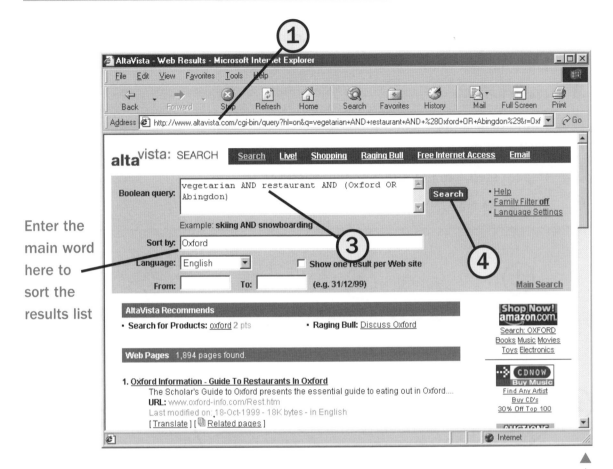

Enter the main word here to sort the results list

▲ ▲ Running an advanced search at AltaVista

Infoseek

At Infoseek you can search by entering one or more words, perhaps linked by logical operators, but this can produce ludicrous numbers of 'matching' pages. A search for 'vegetarian restaurant Oxford' will give you just over 1,000,000 hits – all the pages containing 'vegetarian', plus all those with 'restaurant' plus all those with 'Oxford'.

Infoseek offers a very effective way to find want you want. You can run a series of searches, each based on the results of the last. In the example, we start by entering just one of the keywords – 'vegetarian'. This produced 137,000 hits. Searching through these hits for those that also contained 'restaurant' brought the number down to 3,2000. A final filter with 'Oxford' reduced this to 21 – and about half of these were relevant. (Most of the rest were for Oxfords outside the UK.)

Exploring the World Wide Web

1 Go to Infoseek at: http://infoseek.go.com

2 Enter the first word.

3 Click Find.

4 At the results page, enter the next word, select Search within results and click Find again.

5 Repeat step 4 to get a reasonably-sized set.

6 Follow the links.

The related searches are sometimes worth trying

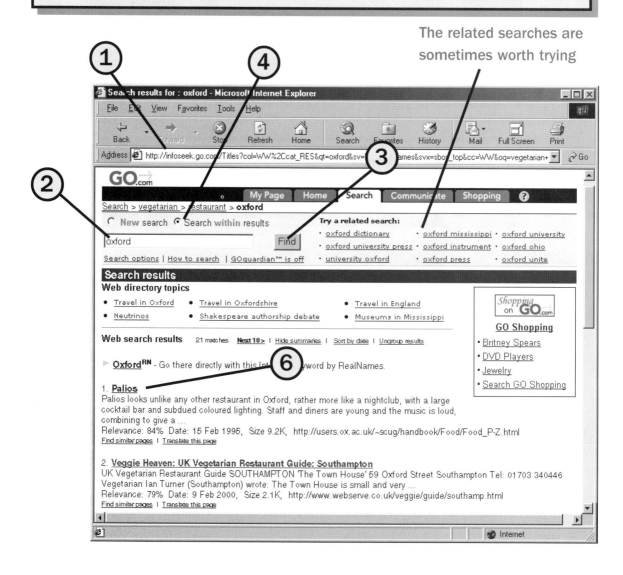

The History list

As you browse, each page is recorded in the History list as an Internet Shortcut – i.e. a link to the page, and its files are stored on your hard drive. Clicking the History button opens the list in the Explorer Bar, where the links are organised into folders, according to site.

If you want to use the History off-line, open the **File** menu and turn on the **Work Offline**. Note that if a page actively draws from its home site – typically to get fresh adverts – you will not be able to open it off-line.

> Off-line – disconnected from the Internet. Browsers and mail software can be run off-line, so that you can revisit stored pages or read and compose messages after you have hung up the phone.

1   Click the History button to open the list in the Explorer Bar.

2   Click the site name or folder icon to open a site's folder.

3   Select the page – if it is 'greyed out', it is not available off-line.

4   Click the X at the top right of the Explorer Bar to close it when you've done.

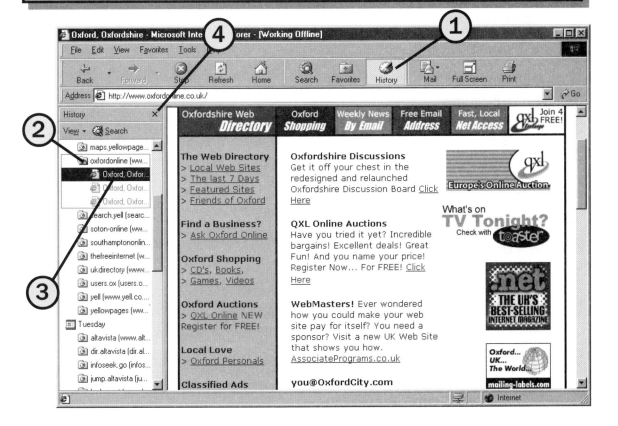

Favorites

Some good places ... you discover after a long and painful search or by sheer chance

Some good places are easy to find; others you discover after a long and painful search or by sheer chance. If you want to return to these pages in future, the simple solution is to add them to your Favorites. This stores the title and URL of the page, and puts the title onto the Favorites menu.

▷ If you want to go back to a page in a later session, you can pick it from the Favorites menu or the Favorites list in the Explorer Bar.

▷ The page must be open to be able to add it to the Favorites – but you can add pages off-line by opening them from the History list.

▷ The Favorites are stored in a folder. If you have a lot of entries, you can organise them into new folders within this, creating submenus of Favorites. It is quicker to open one or two levels of folders than to hunt through a long list.

❑ **Adding Favorites**

1 Find a good page!

2 Open the Favorites menu or open Favorites in the Explorer Bar and select Add to Favorites.

3 Edit the name if necessary.

4 To store it in a folder, click Create in>> and select the folder.

5 Click OK.

❑ **Organising Favorites**

6 Click Organize Favorites.

7 Click on a folder if you need to work on its contents.

8 To move a link within a menu, drag it up or down – a thick line will show you where it will be placed when you release the mouse button.

9 To move a link into a folder, select it, drag it up to the folder and drop it in.

Click to open (and close)
Favorites in the Explorer Bar

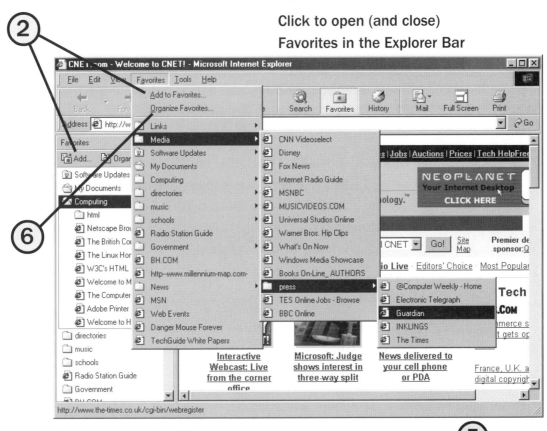

If you don't like 'drag and drop' for
moving links, select the link and click
here then pick a folder from the list

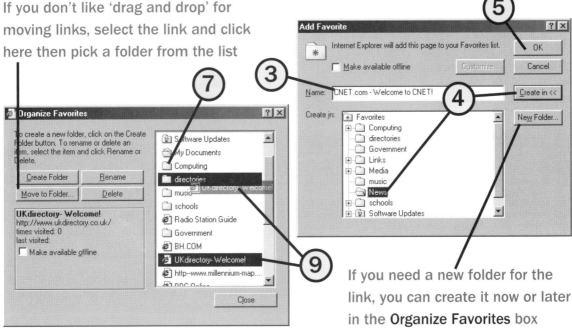

If you need a new folder for the
link, you can create it now or later
in the **Organize Favorites** box

Using Netscape Navigator

Netscape Navigator is the main alternative to IE – it was the leading browser until Microsoft bundled IE in with Windows. It does exactly the same job – slightly better in some respects, slightly worse in others – and has very similar sets of tools and features.

Instead of *Favorites*, Navigator has *Bookmarks* – same thing, different name! They can be grouped into folders/submenus, and organised through the **Edit Bookmarks** routine. When a useful link is found, **Add Bookmark** will add it to the main menu, or **File Bookmark** can be used to select a folder to store it in.

History is handled through a separate window, which can be kept open while you go back over pages.

As Navigator also caches the files from visited pages on the hard drive, you can revisit Bookmarks and History pages offline.

Navigator's History list is displayed
in a separate window
▼
▼

Click a heading to sort into
order by that column

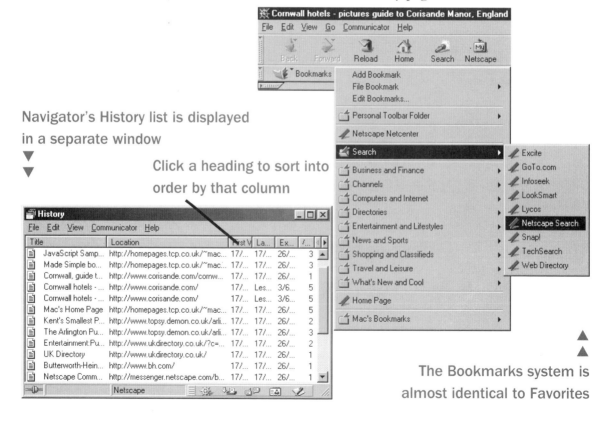

The Bookmarks system is
almost identical to Favorites

4

E-mail

Electronic mail

For many Internet users, e-mail is the most important aspect of the Net, and the one they use most often. Once the initial fascination of the Web has worn off, most people will only go surfing when they are looking for specific information, but they will continue to check their e-mailbox once or twice every day.

E-mail messages are perhaps more more like memos than postal mail. A message can be easily copied to other users; and when you receive an incoming message, you can attach your reply to it, or forward it on to a third party. You can also attach documents and graphics files to messages – so, when you reply to an enquiry from a potential customer, you can send them a copy of your electronic brochure (see *Files by mail*, page 60). E-mail messages can be read and written off-line – this is the cheapest and often the most convenient way of dealing with your mail.

E-mail is fast, cheap and (generally) very reliable.

E-mail is fast, cheap and (generally) very reliable.

▷   It's fast – messages will sometimes get through almost instantaneously, but at worst will be there within a few hours. The delay is because not all of the computers that handle mail are constantly in touch with each other. Instead, they will link up at regular intervals to deal with the mail and other services.

▷   It's cheap – a typical message can be sent in a few seconds and costs virtually nothing in phone time. Attachments will slow things down, but it's still a cheap way to send out documents. A four-page full-colour brochure, for instance, might make a file of around 1Mb. Attached to an e-mail, this would take about 5 minutes to send and cost little more than 5p. (See page 60 for more on this.)

▷   It's reliable – e-mail very, very rarely fails to get through. If you've made a mistake in the e-mail address, then it will be bounced back to you – unless the mistake has turned it into someone else's real address!

E-mail addresses

As with snail mail, to send someone e-mail you need their address. The standard pattern for a person's e-mail address is:

username@companydomain

The **companydomain** may be the person's ISP, company or Web mail service. The **username** may be the person's real name, in one form or another, or may be something completely different. For example, here are four of the e-mail addresses used by the authors.

david@corisande.com

David's address at his hotel's company domain. It's a small domain, and it's his, so 'david' is enough to identify him. In a larger organisation, the normal pattern is **firstname.surname@company**, for example, here's our publisher, **sally.north@repp.co.uk** (Butterworth-Heinemann is part of Reed Educational and Professional Publishing).

corisande2@hotmail

And David's address when he is on holiday – this is a Web mail address (see page 66). He could have used **david.grant@hotmail**, but someone else had got there first! Unless you get in early, or have an unusual name, don't expect to be able to use your normal name with any of the big e-mail providers.

macbride@tcp.co.uk

Mac's normal address at his ISP – Total Connectivity Providers (TCP).

macbride.uk@excite.com

Mac's Web mail address at Excite UK – he did get in early!

There are sites on the Internet that will help you to find people's e-mail addresses (e.g. **http://www.whowhere.com**), but the simplest way is to phone them and ask them to e-mail you! Every message carries its sender's address.

Outlook Express

▼
▼
▼
▼
▼

Outlook Express is simple to use, and easy to set up.

This is the e-mail software that is supplied along with Windows 98 and with Internet Explorer. It is simple to use, and easy to set up.

The first time that you try to use Outlook Express, a Wizard will collect the details that it needs to set up the mail connection. Get this information from your service provider and have it to hand:

▷ Your user name and password

▷ Your e-mail name, e.g. JoSmith@mynet.co.uk

▷ The names of your service provider's Incoming and Outgoing Mail Servers – these may well be the same.

Incoming messages are placed in the Inbox folder, and listed in the Header pane. This shows who they are from, their Subject, date sent and other indicators. Clicking on a message header will open the message in the Preview Pane, if present, or in a separate message window.

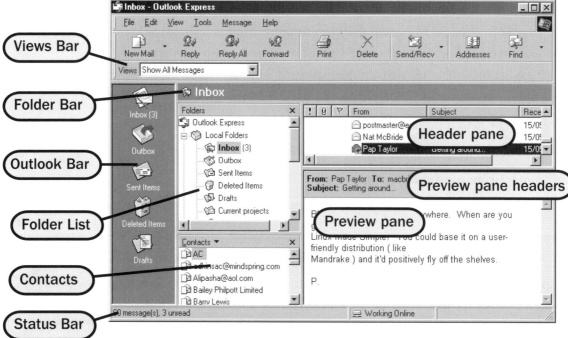

The Preview Pane can be below or to the right, or turned off

View options

The **View** menu gives you wide-ranging control over the appearance of the window. The crucial settings are the **Layout** options, which determine the components to be displayed. The only fixed part is the Header pane. Contacts, the Outlook Bar, Views Bar, Folder Bar, Status Bar, Folder List, Toolbar and Preview Pane are all optional. As the Folder List and Outlook Bars both do the same job, keep whichever you prefer.

1   Open the View menu, select Layout...

2   In the Basic set, click on the boxes to turn the components on or off.

3   In the Preview Pane area, select if and where you want the Preview Pane.

4   Click OK.

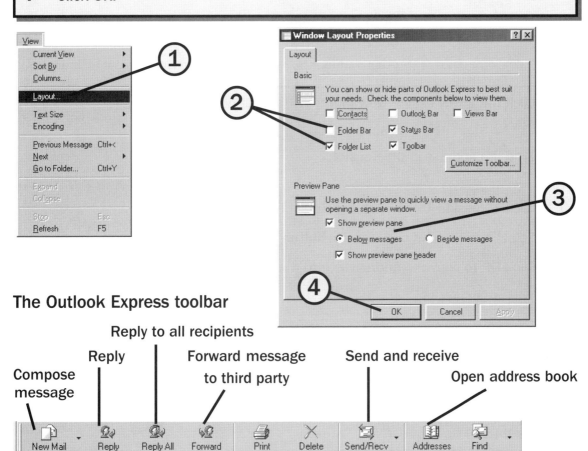

The Outlook Express toolbar

Reply to all recipients

Reply

Forward message
to third party

Send and receive

Compose
message

Open address book

New Mail | Reply | Reply All | Forward | Print | Delete | Send/Recv | Addresses | Find

Sending messages

▼
▼
▼
▼
▼

To send e-mail, all
you need is the
address – and
something to say!

To send e-mail, all you need is the address – and something to say! Messages can be written and sent immediately if you are on-line, or written off-line and stored for sending later.

To add impact, write your message on appropriate stationery! These have text formats and backgrounds all ready for you.

When you send mail, there are three categories of recipients, and you can have as many as you like in each category:

▷ **To:** the ones for whom the message is primarily intended – you would normally expect a reply from these;

▷ **Cc:** (Carbon copies), sent for information, rather than action;

▷ **Bcc:** (Blind carbon copies) – the recipients are not listed on the other copies. Use these where recipients should not see each other's addresses, e.g. when sending circulars out to your clients.

1 Click the arrow beside New Mail 🗋▾ and select your stationery.

❑ Use No stationery – or simply click 🗋 for plain paper.

2 Type the address in the To: slot.

or

3 Click 📖 beside To: to open the Select Recipients dialog box.

4 Select a name and click the To: button or the Cc: or Bcc: buttons.

5 Click OK to copy the addresses into the message and close the dialog box.

6 Type a Subject.

7 Type your message.

8 Click 📤 the Send button.

or

9 Open the File menu and select Send Message, for immediate delivery, or Send Later.

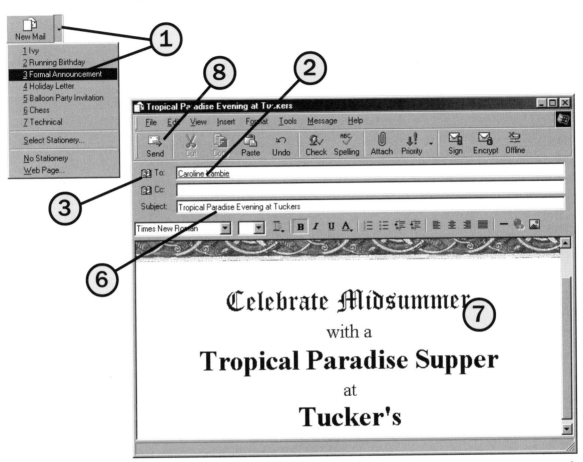

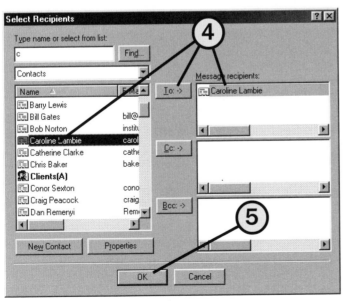

Writing a new message in Outlook Express. If you use stationery, or the Rich Text (HTML) format, you can format messages, as in a word-processor. The Plain Text format produces much smaller message files, which take less phone time to send and receive.

Use the **Format** menu to switch between **Rich Text** and **Plain Text**.

Replying

When you reply to an incoming message, the system will open the New message window and copy the sender's address into the **To**: text box.

The original message is normally also copied into the main text area with > at the start of each line. This can be very handy if you want to respond to the mail point-by-point. Any unwanted parts of the message can be deleted, and you can insert your own text before, after or between the original lines.

If you don't want the message copied in, go to the **Options** dialog box (from the **Tools** menu), switch to the **Send** tab and turn **Include message in reply** off.

Reply to all

If you get a message that has been sent to several people, you can reply to all those listed in the **To:** and **Cc:** boxes. Click **Reply to All**, instead of **Reply to Sender**, and continue as for a normal reply. Your message will be copied to all the recipients of the original message.

Forwarding messages

You can also send a message on to another person – perhaps after adding your own comments to it.

1	Select the message in the header pane.
2	Click Reply to All, Reply to Sender or Forward
3	If forwarding, type or select the address(es) of the recipient(s).
4	Delete any unwanted headers or other text and add your own comments.
5	Click Send.

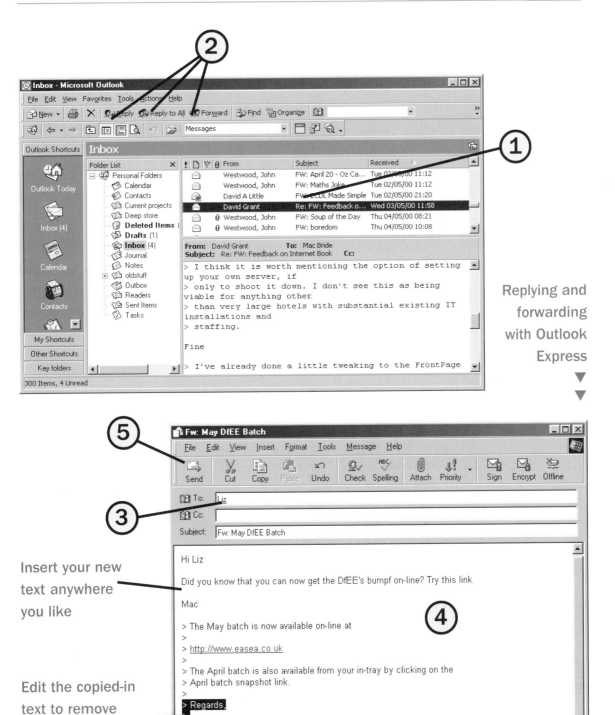

Replying and
forwarding
with Outlook
Express

Insert your new
text anywhere
you like

Edit the copied-in
text to remove
unwanted lines

Files by mail

Files of any type – images, word-processor documents, spreadsheets, audio clips or whatever – can be attached to messages and sent by e-mail. Compared to sending files as printouts or on disks in the post, e-mail is almost always quicker, often more reliable and usually much cheaper.

Use this method to send brochures to your Website's visitors who want more details, or to inform past/regular clients of special events or offers.

When files are attached to messages, they have to be converted into a special format for transmission through the e-mail system. This is not something that you have to worry about – Outlook Express, like all modern e-mail software, handles the conversion for you – but you should be aware that it makes files about 50% bigger. So, if you had a brochure file of 1Mb, it would produce an e-mail message of around 1.5Mb. E-mail typically transfers at between 3Kb and 5Kb per second, or 2–300Kb a minute, so this brochure would take 5 to 7 minutes to send.

It will also, of course, take just as long to receive. Take care, there is potential here for antagonising clients! If you send someone an e-mail, they must receive it – they don't have to read it, but they do have to download it from their e-mailbox at their ISP. Don't send big files without warning. If the file will take more than a few minutes to transfer, then store it on a page at your Website and simply e-mail a link to it, telling the recipient what it is and how big it is.

1   Start to write the message as normal.

2   Click 🔘 Attach File or open the Insert menu and select File Attachment.

3   Browse for the file and click Attach.

4   Finish the message and send it.

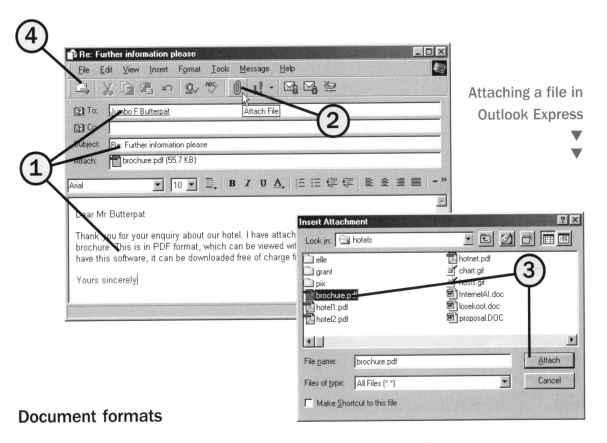

Attaching a file in
Outlook Express

Document formats

If you want to produce nicely laid-out, illustrated documents in a file format that most people can read, there are two prime choices:

▷   Microsoft Word 6.0 (or earlier) format. Word is by far the most commonly-used word-processor, but not everyone has the latest version. Word 6.0 files can be read by all later Words – and by most other word-processors produced in the last few years.

▷   PDF – Portable Document Format – files can be viewed on any computer or printed on any printer as long as the right software is present. On a PC, you need Acrobat Reader. This can be downloaded free from Adobe, at **http://www.adobe.com**. To produce PDF files, you need Acrobat Distiller which can be bought separately, or as part of a DTP package from Adobe.

As a general rule, a brochure in PDF format could look better and make a smaller file than a Word document.

Address Book

Typing e-mail addresses is a pain – one slip and the mail comes bouncing back with a 'recipient unknown' label. The simple solution is to use the Address Book. Type the address in once correctly – or add it from an incoming message (use **Tools > Add Sender to Address Book**) – and it's there whenever you want it.

1 Click the Address Book button 📖 .

2 Click 📇 New and select New Contact.

3 Enter the First, Middle and Last names, and edit the Display name if you don't want the full one.

4 Type the e-mail address and click [Add].

5 If the person has several addresses, add them and set one as the Default.

6 Click OK.

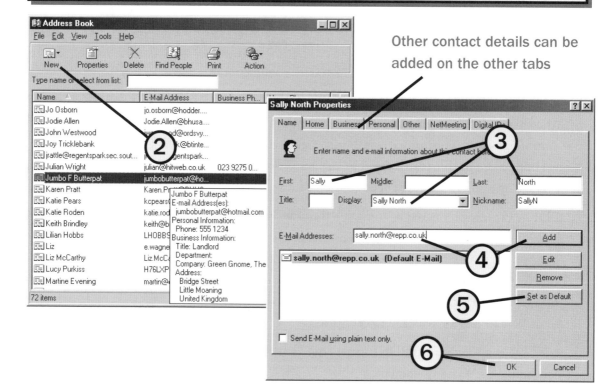

Other contact details can be added on the other tabs

Group mailings

The same e-mail message can be sent to any number of people at the same time. You can do this by adding the addresses one by one to the **To:** or **Cc:** recipient lists, but if you are regularly sending mail to the same set of people there is a better way. The Address Book will let you define a set of addresses as a named *group*. When you want to write to those people, you simply select the group as the recipient.

1 Click [New] and select New Group.

2 Type a name for the group.

3 Click [Select Members].

4 Select a member and click [Select ->], repeating to add all the group.

5 Click OK to close the Select Group Members dialog box.

6 Click OK to close the Properties box – to reopen it for editing, double-click on the group's name in the Address Book.

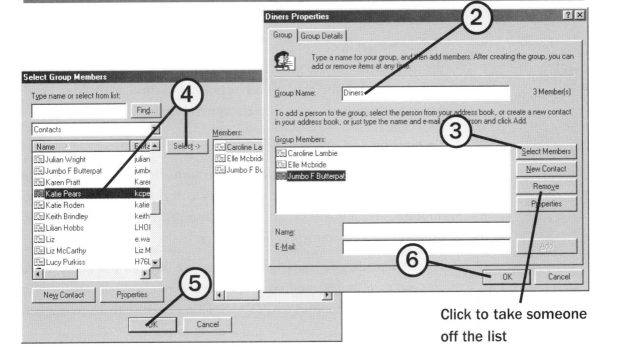

Click to take someone off the list

E-mail etiquette

When you send someone a paper letter, you know that what they receive will be the same as you send, and if you enclose lots of material, you will pay the extra postage. E-mail is different. Your recipients actively download your messages, which takes time and can cost money. Further, if they are using different mail software to yours, it can affect the appearance – and sometimes the *delivery* – of your messages.

Size

Some e-mail systems set a limit to the size of messages, typically 1000 lines (roughly 70Kb). You are hardly likely to write this much, but an attached file can easily push the message size over the limit. Even where there is no limit, file size is still a factor. The larger the file, the longer it takes to download, and the higher your recipients' phone bills.

Use the standard WinZip software to compress data files before attaching them. Graphics and documents files can be reduced to 10% or less of their original size this way.

Subject lines

A clear Subject line identifies a message. Your recipients need this when the mail arrives, to see which to deal with first – and which to ignore completely! They also need it when organising old mail, so that they know which to delete and which to place in what folder.

Formatting and emphasis

Most modern e-mail software can display formatted text, but few people bother with formatting. The essence of e-mail is that it is quick and informal – plain text is very much the norm. Save your fancy stationery for special announcements and greetings.

If you are sending formatted text, you can use **bold** for emphasis. If you are sending plain text, and want to make a word stand out, enclose it in *asterisks* or write it in CAPITALS. Don't overuse these. Writing in capitals is known as *shouting* – and is tiring to read.

Smileys

E-mail messages tend to be brief, and as your receipients cannot see your expression or hear the tone of your voice, there is a possibility of being misunderstood – especially when joking. Smileys, also known as *emoticons,* are little pictures, composed of ASCII characters, that can help to convey your meaning.

The basic smiley of **:–)** is the one you will see most often, though there are many other weird and wonderful smileys around. Here are a few of the more common ones.

> :-) **It's a joke**
>
> '-) **Wink**
>
> :-(**I'm feeling sad**
>
> :-o **Wow!**
>
> :-C **I don't believe it!**
>
> (-: **I'm left handed**

Abbreviations

If you are an indifferent typist, or like to keep your messages short, or are likely to be getting mail from old 'netties', then it's worth learning a few of the standard abbreviations. You will also find these used in real-time conferences and chat lines, and in newsgroup articles.

BTW   By The Way

BWQ   Buzz Word Quotient

FYI   For Your Information

IMHO   In My Humble Opinion (ironic)

MOTSS Member Of The Same Sex

POV   Point Of View

TIA   Thanks In Advance

TTFN   Ta Ta For Now

WRT   With Reference To

<g>   Grin

Learning Resources
Centre

Web mail

Go to almost any of the major directories and you will be offered free 'Web mail' – an e-mail service based at a Web site not at an ISP.

The crucial difference between Web mail and ordinary e-mail is that the mail folders, where messages are stored, are on-line. With normal e-mail, you only need to be on-line while you are sending and receiving messages – they can be read and written, moved and deleted off-line. With Web mail, you must (normally) be on-line the whole time that you are dealing with your mail. (It is possible to download messages for reading and storage, and to transfer up to the site, messages that you have written in a word-processor.) As a result, dealing with the mail is slower – and more costly if you are paying for the on-line and telephone time.

The big advantage of Web mail – apart from the fact that it is free – is that you can access your mailbox from anywhere as long as you can get into the Internet somehow. This may be through a terminal in a public library, from a friend's or colleague's desktop anywhere in the world, or through your own (temporary) account at your place of work or study.

An increasing number of your guests will have Web mail addresses and will appreciate access to the Net from your hotel

You may find it useful to get yourself a Web mail address if you want to keep in touch while you are away. More to the point, if you are running a hotel, you should realise that an increasing number of your guests will have Web mail addresses and will therefore appreciate access to the Net from your hotel. This is not difficult or costly to arrange – all it takes is an extra Internet account (with a free ISP?) and a PC that guests can use.

Sign up for a Web mail address and play with it, to get the hang of what it is all about. Some Web mail providers are:

MailCity	www.mailcity.com
Excite	mail.excite.com
Yahoo	mail.yahoo.com
Netcenter	home.netcenter.com

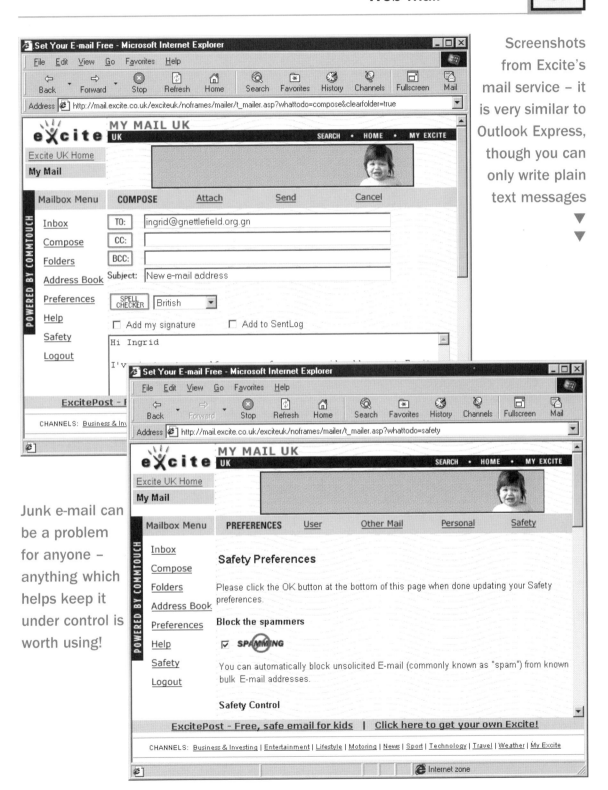

Screenshots from Excite's mail service – it is very similar to Outlook Express, though you can only write plain text messages ▼ ▼

Junk e-mail can be a problem for anyone – anything which helps keep it under control is worth using!

5

Why think about 'going on-line'?

▼
▼
▼
▼
▼

What does 'going on-line' mean?

You are losing money today if your business is not on-line.

There are two key aspects to this:

▷ Having your own Web site.

▷ Corresponding with your customers by e-mail.

We set out in this book to try to cut away the mystique and jargon, and give you enough background on the world of cyberspace to enable you to decide which of many routes you can go down, from the simple option of a one-page site on a larger commercial site – to creating your own site with lots of pages – to any of the options in between.

There are, as we noted earlier, around 300 million people across the world connected to the Internet. However, if you are marketing on the Web, you need to realise that very few of these 300 million will ever find an individual Web site from the millions of sites available out there in cyberspace. Nevertheless, a great many people are looking at this very moment on the Internet for the product that you are selling.

> Surfer – someone moving through the Web, viewing pages.

Without a Web site these surfers will never buy from you. They are part of a new breed who will only buy if they can find it on the Net. These are not all young trendy, computer-literate people. They can equally be retired civil servants living in Middle America, or carpenters living in Cornwall.

There are three parts to the equation:

▶ First the Web surfer has to find your Web site

▶ Then they have stay on your Web site long enough to read it

▶ Then they will correspond with you by e-mail, probably a couple of times, before deciding to buy.

To be in the game you must understand the background to each part of this conundrum.

How do people find your site?

How does someone living in Colorado or Cardiff find a hotel to stay in Cornwall?

To answer this question you need to understand a bit about search engines and directories.

It is important to realise that a few search engines and directories are far, far more popular than the rest, so it is irrelevant that your site is registered on 500 search engines. To find the answer to our question the Web surfer will in all probability go to Yahoo, AltaVista or Infoseek. They will then type a query into the 'find' box.

This example shows what the surfer gets if the just type 'Cornwall' into AltaVista.

What 'Cornwall' will find at AltaVista

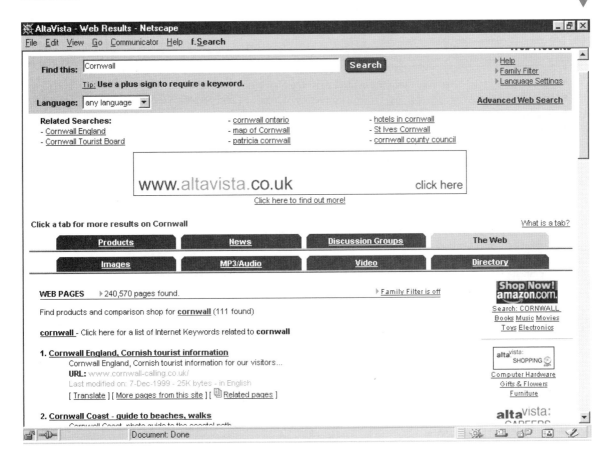

If the user was to type 'Cornwall hotels' or 'a hotel in Cornwall' or 'Cornish accommodation' or whatever other permutation you could think of, then Alta Vista would give a completely different list. And if the user had interrogated Excite, Infoseek, HotBot or any other search engine, then they would have got different lists still.

The good news is that you can influence your search engine placing by clever writing of your Web site, but the bad news is that not all search engines will rank you as high for the same page, nor can you ensure that you will be maximised for all possible keywords that you may be searched for under.

The Yahoo listings will bring you a lot of visitors – if Yahoo accepts your site
▼
▼

Directories work differently, the searcher inputs a query, and gets taken to a category in the directory. In this example at Yahoo the query was for 'Cornwall hotels', and no matter what permutation of words you try, you will get the same directory page.

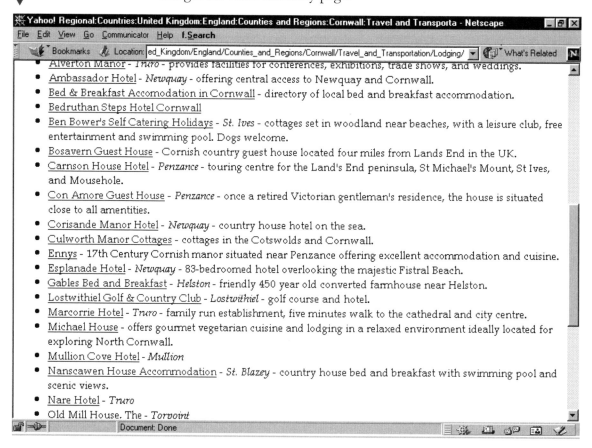

Yahoo! Regional:Countries:United Kingdom:England:Counties and Regions:Cornwall:Travel and Transporta - Netscape

File Edit View Go Communicator Help f.Search

Bookmarks   Location: ed_Kingdom/England/Counties_and_Regions/Cornwall/Travel_and_Transportation/Lodging/   What's Related

- Alverton Manor - *Truro* - provides facilities for conferences, exhibitions, trade shows, and weddings.
- Ambassador Hotel - *Newquay* - offering central access to Newquay and Cornwall.
- Bed & Breakfast Accomodation in Cornwall - directory of local bed and breakfast accommodation.
- Bedruthan Steps Hotel Cornwall
- Ben Bower's Self Catering Holidays - *St. Ives* - cottages set in woodland near beaches, with a leisure club, free entertainment and swimming pool. Dogs welcome.
- Bosavern Guest House - Cornish country guest house located four miles from Lands End in the UK.
- Carnson House Hotel - *Penzance* - touring centre for the Land's End peninsula, St Michael's Mount, St Ives, and Mousehole.
- Con Amore Guest House - *Penzance* - once a retired Victorian gentleman's residence, the house is situated close to all amentities.
- Corisande Manor Hotel - *Newquay* - country house hotel on the sea.
- Culworth Manor Cottages - cottages in the Cotswolds and Cornwall.
- Ennys - 17th Century Cornish manor situated near Penzance offering excellent accommodation and cuisine.
- Esplanade Hotel - *Newquay* - 83-bedroomed hotel overlooking the majestic Fistral Beach.
- Gables Bed and Breakfast - *Helston* - friendly 450 year old converted farmhouse near Helston.
- Lostwithiel Golf & Country Club - *Lostwithiel* - golf course and hotel.
- Marcorrie Hotel - *Truro* - family run establishment, five minutes walk to the cathedral and city centre.
- Michael House - offers gourmet vegetarian cuisine and lodging in a relaxed environment ideally located for exploring North Cornwall.
- Mullion Cove Hotel - *Mullion*
- Nanscawen House Accommodation - *St. Blazey* - country house bed and breakfast with swimming pool and scenic views.
- Nare Hotel - *Truro*
- Old Mill House, The - *Torpoint*

Document: Done

The good news is that once you get on Yahoo it will direct a great deal of Web traffic to your site, the bad news is that you have no control over whether they list you, or what they say about your site. To get considered by Yahoo, you must submit your site and accept that they may well not get round to even looking at the site.

If you are running a pub or restaurant, or a hotel that caters also for the local market, find out if your town has its own local information/ advertising site. You can normally add a link to your own Web site for free, and advertising rates are usually very low.

If all or part of your market is local, make sure you are listed in local sites
▼
▼

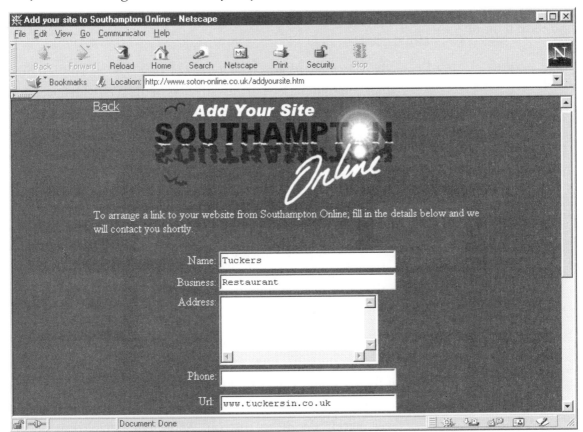

And don't forget Yell (page 38). People are increasingly using Yell, rather than the paper Yellow Pages, to look up businesses, both in their local area and further afield.

Keeping visitors on-site

You have to grab them long enough to make them stop and read a bit of your site.

Having found it, they have to be attracted enough to your site to stay to at least read it. The whole essence of surfing the Internet is that there is the freedom to click quickly from one site to the next using either hyperlinks or the Back button on the browser.

So when a surfer reaches your site, they may have looked at 50 pages already that day, and have the intention to look at 50 more. Therefore you have to grab them long enough to make them stop and read a bit of your site. A few of the things that may make the visitor **not** bother stopping are:

▷   *An empty page with nothing on it that says 'click to enter'.* This is a tired marketing gimmick from the early days of the Web with fewer sites around. The thought behind it is that if they clicked to enter, then they were making a positive commitment to enter. There is little truth in that today. Seeing that page may well make them surf straight on.

▷   *A slow server.* That is, the provider of your Web space cannot supply information fast enough on all the sites that they are hosting, so they have to ration the supply of information by cutting the speed of sending out data. Your Web site visitor will experience this by a very slow download of your site to their computer. You can see for yourself slow downloads if you visit some of the free sites.

▷   *A slow site.* This is different from a slow server above, though the effect for the surfer is the same. If your page has too much data on it then it will take ages to download, and the visitor may well be looking at an empty screen while this is happening. Most surfers will quickly decide to surf on. A big photograph can be the problem, and has to be got round by making it electronically 'fuzzier', taking out data from the photo to make it download quicker.

▷   *An uninteresting front page* will obviously make the visitor loathe to loiter.

Your first page must have a graphical way of quickly telling the surfer that they really should stop now and look at this site. This can be achieved with a mixture of photographs and selling points. By showing at a glance what you are all about, you avoid wasting the surfers' time if they are not interested, but succeed in attracting them if they are.

Sell them your product

The first objective of slowing the frenetic Web surfer down, and getting them to look at your site is difficult, but if achieved, then you have the chance to sell. Selling is achieved two ways:

▷   from the information on the site

▷   from dealing with e-mail enquiries

After the front page, fast downloading and doing a brutal selling job, you can add as much detail as you like to the other pages on the site. Photographs can take longer to download if you think the visitor actually needs a big photograph at that stage of their visit. Pages can cover more peripheral information like events in the area, personal touches like photographs of the proprietor walking his dog, or the chef's recipe for Yorkshire pudding. Talk to existing and potential guests, or put yourself into their shoes, to try to see what information they might need before booking, and aim to provide it for them.

You can add as much detail as you like to the other pages on the site

If they like your business, then the Internet surfers may well send you one or more e-mails to clarify their doubts. Inevitably these will involve price and how to find you even though your Web site will cover these items. They may want to know your thoughts on children, dogs, vegetarians, motor cyclists, the number of stairs in your building, whether you speak French, do discounts for groups…

The thing about e-mail is that the enquirer wants an answer, not tomorrow, not even in an hour's time, they want the answer **now**. If you do not answer all your e-mails three or four times a day, then the chances are that someone else will, and the prospective customer will already have bought by the time your tardy reply wings its way to them. Americans in particular are bemused by British hotels not replying to an e-mail and posting a brochure that arrives three weeks later, by which point they have long since booked their entire holiday.

How about on-line bookings?

If your Web site has really sold them your product, can you get them to book immediately on-line? The answer is a big maybe, and with reservations! In the last couple of years, people have become more willing to make credit card transactions over the Internet – it is no riskier than a telephone or mail order purchase. But making a hotel booking is not a simple purchase. Some people will commit directly – and Americans seem to be more willing to do so than Europeans – but in general, potential clients will want to check rates, availability and other details, by e-mail, fax or phone, before making a booking.

Now, any on-line credit card transaction must be done through a secure connection – one where the data is encrypted so that even if a hacker was able to 'eavesdrop', the credit card details would still be safe. Normal Web space is not secure, but your ISP may offer a secure facility for an extra charge. There are also firms that specialise in renting Web space for on-line transactions. To use these, you would set up a booking form at the secure site, and link this from your own site.

If this sounds too much trouble, you might consider using one of the growing number of on-line booking firms, such as the London-based **Web-hotels.com** or the Scottish Hotels booking service (**www.scottish-hotel-breaks.com**). These will market your product, take bookings or direct e-mail enquiries on to you for processing.

But don't rush. At present, individual hotels – certainly outside London – are unlikely to get enough booking on-line to make it worth while.

At Web-hotels, the potential client can read about the hotel, then either ask for more details or make a booking by e-mail, fax or Web form – all through secure connections   ▶▶▶

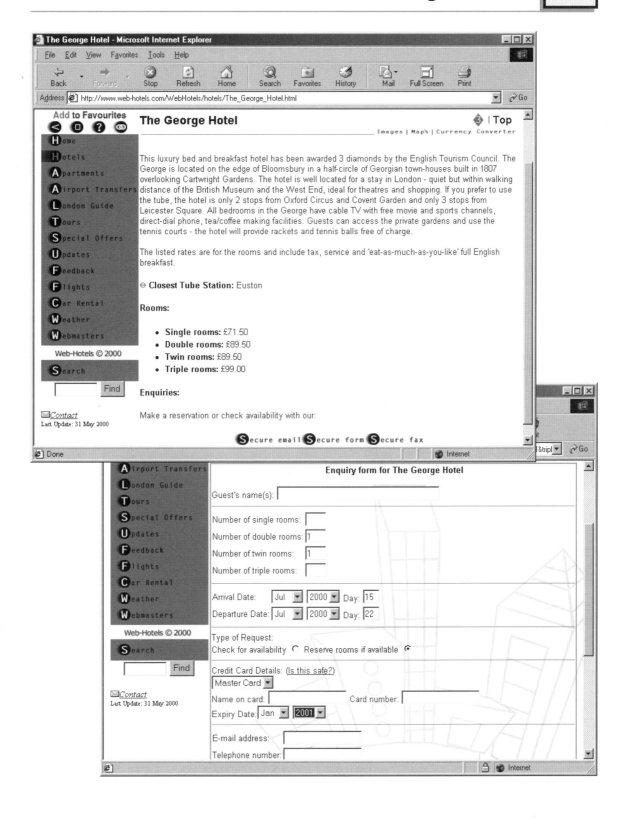

Does it matter how you get on-line?

If you were placing an advert in a small local newspaper, it would cost less, and also been seen by fewer people, than a colour page in a national Sunday newspaper.

The Internet works a bit like that, a page on a big site like the BTA Web site, will never bring you the amount of traffic that having your own site with its own domain name will bring.

Here and on the next pages are three Web sites for Corisande Manor – one on the BTA site, one on Smooth Hound, and one our own site. At first glance one may well ask what is the difference.

Part of Corisande's page at the BTA site

▷   Our BTA page is one of 25,000 accommodations on their database, and supplies limited information to the surfer.

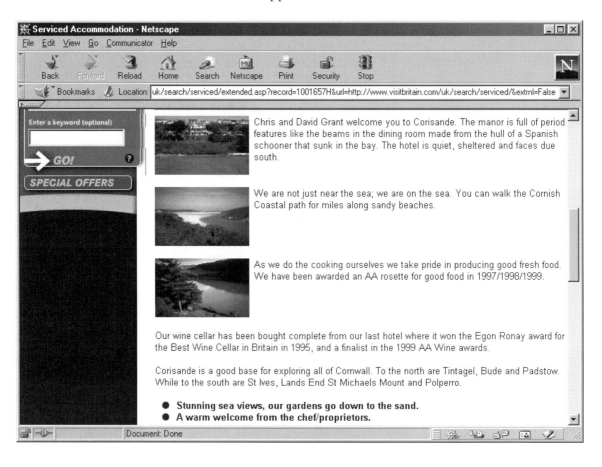

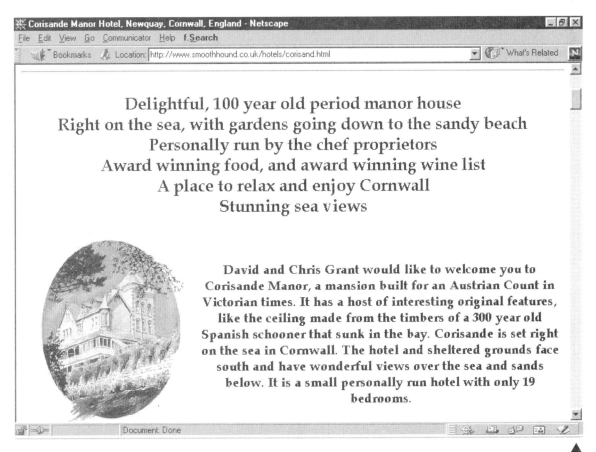

Corisande's page at
Smooth Hound

▷ The Smooth Hound site contains all of our printed brochure, and more. However it is one of 8000 other sites on Smooth Hound.

▷ Our own site has its own Web address (URL) , can be found easily by searchers looking for a hotel in Cornwall directly from search engines without going via other sites.

Many more people will look at the site with its own URL, but it will cost more to maintain and market a site like that than the simpler page on the BTA site, or the Smooth Hound page.

In the course of this book we will try to explain the differences between these types of site, the costs involved and how you procure the various options.

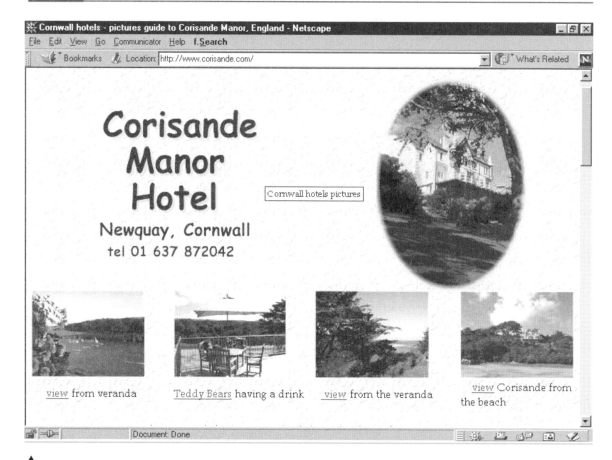

▲
▲
The top page of our
own Web site

Deciding how to get a Web site

Before you do anything on the Web, you should make yourself familiar
with how the whole thing works. Use a browser for a few hours and see
how search engines work and what your competition are doing.

To show you what we mean, if you own a hotel in, for example, Wales:

▷   Go to AltaVista and Excite. Try various combinations of keywords
to see what sites come up. Look at those sites and see who owns
then and has designed them. Browsers will use all combinations,
so you need to look at 'Wales' and 'Welsh', at 'hotel' and 'hotels',
at 'accommodation' and 'lodgings', at 'Snowdon' and 'Snowdonia', and so on.

▷ Go to Yahoo and look at their listings for Welsh hotels. There may be 60 hotels, but you will find it instructive to look at all their sites. Think all the time, if you were looking for a hotel in Wales, which of these would you stay at, on the evidence of their Web site.

▷ Look at the big sites like BTA and AA. See whether you think a surfer in Sacramento would use them to book a hotel

▷ Look at a few Web designers' sites, see which clients they have written for, and check how successful they are at search engine placing for these clients. In other words go to a search engine and try to find their clients with the sort of words you think a tourist would use.

The purpose of these exercises is to make you reasonably aware of what the Internet is all about before you start to get involved in your own site.

How much are you prepared to spend?

This is not quite the £64,000 question – it shouldn't cost you that much – but you do need to think about your budget at a very early stage.

These figures are for guidance only, and are based on typical costs in summer 2000

▷ Investing under £100 a year will get you a page on a big site. It may well bring enough bookings to cover your costs, but is unlikely to have patrons queuing up at the front door of your business.

▷ £1000 is what you are likely to have to spend if you get a Web designer to design, publish, register with search engines, and maintain a site of several pages. Going on from there you can get a more complex site with whistles and bells, Web cameras and sound, for as large a sum as you want. There will always be someone happy to spend your money for you.

▷ You can build your own site for anything from nothing, using free Web space and free software, to around £400 to buy software like FrontPage, register your own domain name and use commercial Web space that delivers fast downloads.

This is not an either-or decision. There is nothing to stop you from having pages at any number of sites, plus your own professionally designed or hand-made site. In the early stages, it may be worth trying out a number of different strategies to see how they work for you.

So, you've decided to have a Web site...

We will show you the various options involved and how to find companies to do it for you, or if you want to write and maintain a site yourself, then we show you how to do that.

We would like to feel that by the time you have read this book, that you will be aware of the choices available to you, the costs and the pitfalls involved.

Delay in having a Web presence is losing you customers

Whatever way you decide to take your own business onto the Internet, our advice is to do it sooner rather than later. Delay in having a Web presence is losing you customers. The technology is not difficult and sooner or later you will have to learn to e-mail and use search engines. Why not make the decision now?

6

Web site marketing

It is a mixture of skill and luck that enables surfers to find your site

The good news is that the Web is very democratic, so a small hotel is just as likely to be found by surfers on the Internet as a large hotel.

Throwing more money on Web positioning does not necessarily get you many more Web site visitors. On the Internet it is a mixture of skill and luck that enables surfers to find your site, rather than the millions of other similar sites out there in cyberspace.

In this chapter we will tell you:

▷   How to find a domain name for your site

▷   How to submit your site to search engines

▷   How to analyse the visits to your site.

If Internet users cannot find your site then they cannot buy your product.

Domain names

The first thing you need is a 'domain name' or 'URL' (Uniform Resource Locator).

Why have your own URL?

There are many answers to that question

▷   It looks more professional and gives a better image.

▷   People can remember a simple URL like 'www.corisande.com' rather than a more complicated one like 'www.123www.co.uk/ seymourhouse/index.html'.

▷   Search engines preferentially index what are called 'top level' domains, for example 'www.corisande.com', over the sub-pages of a domain. And in the case of some free sites with perhaps thousands of individual sites on that server, the search engines will simply not list the individual sites.

▷   Search engines can give a weighting to any keywords in the domain name.

What are these things, URLs anyway?

Look on a URL as a sort of personalised number plate. Every Web site exists at a numeric address like '195.172.86.102'. This is the spot in cyberspace where, in this case, you will find 'www.stmartinshotel.co.uk'.

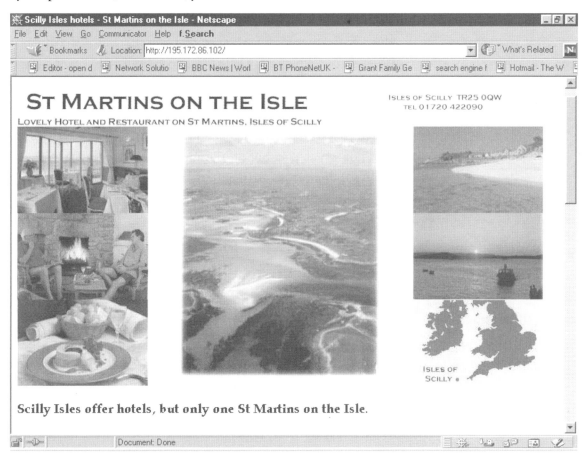

Scilly Isles offer hotels, but only one St Martins on the Isle.

As surfers are unlikely to remember that sort of illogical number, it is obviously better to have a name instead. You register your name with the controlling body, Network Solutions (see page 86), to ensure that every URL is unique. Once your name is registered, computers in cyberspace, called 'Name Servers', translate the request for 'www.stmartinshotel.co.uk' to '195.172.86.102', and seamlessly send surfers on to the correct destination, without them being aware of what is happening.

If you try it, you will see that typing either the name or the number into your browser's location box, will lead you to St Martins Hotel Web site.

▲

▲

No Web site has to have a name, but it sure helps – could you remember the ULR numbers for this site!

Web site marketing

How do you get your own URL?

The most common choice is between '.com' and '.co.uk'. Why choose one rather than the other? There is never a straightforward answer to this – more a question of seeing where you come out on a checklist of swings and roundabouts.

▷　'dot com' is seen as perhaps more international than 'dot co dot uk'. Whereas the 'dot co dot uk' is more specifically UK-oriented, and is perhaps better if you are wanting to make sure your prospective customers realise that you are a UK company.

I liked the sound and simplicity of 'www.corisande.com' for my own hotel Web site, but St Martins Hotel needed a UK URL to show surfers it was in Britain and not a hotel on the Caribbean Island called St Martins.

Simpler domain names are better – especially if you have to give them out over the phone

▷　'dot com' addresses are easier for you to give out on the phone, particularly if the URL itself is a bit involved. The first Web site I ever wrote was 'www.cornwall-calling.co.uk' and I soon realised that it was a bit tricky for people to grasp over the phone. So I registered 'www.corisande.com' as our hotel URL in order to have a very simple Web address to give enquirers.

▷　It also depends on what names are available. As the Web has seen explosive growth, more and more of the short names are used up. Even names you would never think would have been registered.

Maes-y-Neuadd hotel could not register 'maes.com' someone had taken it already. They decided on 'neuadd.com' as an acceptable alternative. Pen-y-Dyffryn Hotel could not register 'dyffryn.co.uk', and settled on 'peny.co.uk'

Popular names obviously have been taken. The White House Hotel in Cheshire, not unnaturally, found it could not register 'www.white-house.com' as the US President had got there first, and took 'www.cheshire-white-house.com' as their domain name.

How do you find out what names are available ?

To find what names have been registered, go to Network Solutions.

1 Go to the address http://www.networksolutions.com/

2 Click the link to the Who is page.

3 Type the domain name that you would like into the box they give you.

4 Hit the Search button. If the name is already registered, you will be told to whom it is registered in case you want to try to buy it from them.

Looking up corisande.com at
Network Solutions

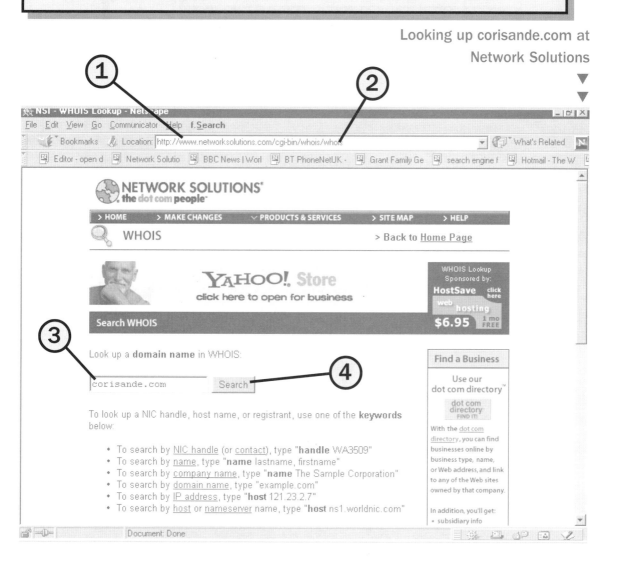

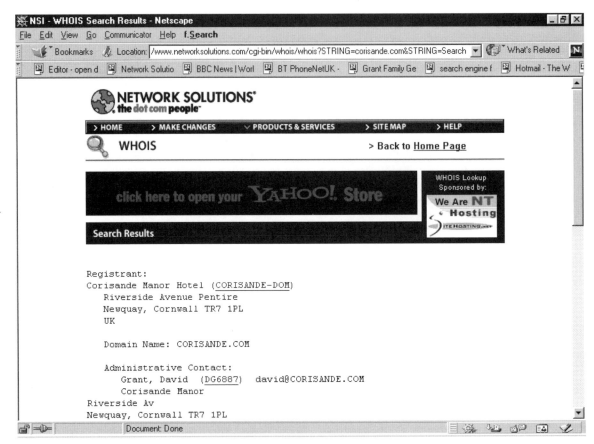

▲
▲
If a name is already registered, you will be told who owns it

Network Solutions are the 'dot com' people. The 'dot co dot uk' people, Nominet UK, at **http://www.nic.uk/whois.html** operate in a very similar way. You just fill in the enquiry box, and in seconds you will see if anyone has registered that name already. You have to be creative in trying all sorts of names, as many names have by now been registered.

With a little bit of thought you can find an acceptable name. In this example, I tried to see if 'BritainsBestHotel.co.uk' was registered. Back came the answer that there was 'no match' for my query, which means that I could register this very desirable name straight away.

If it is not registered already by someone else, then you can register your choice on-line. Just fill up a form on their Web site with your credit card details, and within seconds you are the owner of a gleaming new URL.

You have registered your URL and got a site up and running – what next?

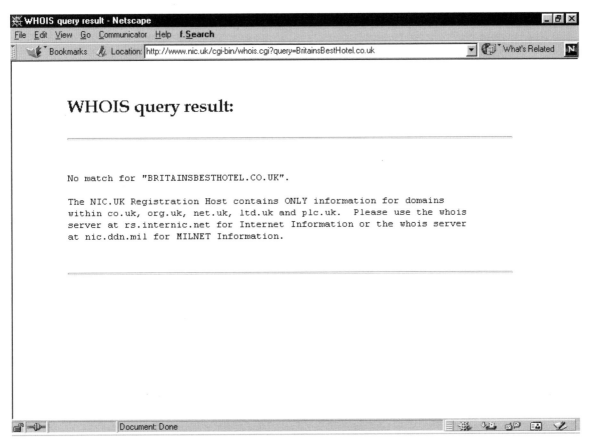

How do search engines find your site?

It is very unlikely that a search engine will just happen to find your Web site, you have to let the search engine know that it is there. Let us show you how that is done, how to register as a supplicant to a search engine, and how they go about putting you on their database.

First, note that directories and search engines operate in different ways.

> This desirable domain name was available – but it's probably gone now

Directories

A directory is a database that is operated by humans. Before listing, a site is reviewed by a human editor.

The principal directories are Yahoo and the Open Directory (used by many search engines as a backup source of information). You submit and

A listing on Yahoo
will bring a marked
increase in the
traffic to your site

hope that the human editor reviewing your site will be sufficiently impressed to include it in the directory.

However, particularly on Yahoo, the limited number of editors and the high number of sites submitted means that they only will review a portion of sites submitted and the rest never get looked at and just disappear off the waiting list for review after a period. Nobody – no professional Web designer, no search engine marketer, nobody – can guarantee that Yahoo will even look at your site, let alone review it and list it. Perhaps Yahoo is not quite as important as it was a year ago, but none the less, a listing on Yahoo will bring a marked increase in the traffic to your site. Further, Yahoo will bring more traffic than any other search engine or directory.

If you do not get an e-mail from them saying that you have been listed, then all you can do is resubmit every week if your site has not been added.

To submit a site to Yahoo is a little complicated, but if you follow the rules they set, the process is fairly straightforward. The Open Directory, and other directories, have very similar ways of accepting sites.

It is vital that you submit to the correct category. Remember that there are too many submissions for the editors to really handle. Therefore you must find the right place in their directory for your site to be listed.

1   To find the right place, carry out a search using the keywords that you would expect people to use to find your business. For example, try a search for a hotel in 'Snowdonia, Wales'.

2   When the answer comes up, right at the bottom of the page of hotels that Yahoo have already listed, you will see a link for Suggest a Site.

3   Click that link, and you get taken to the page for the add-on process.

4   Follow their instructions through three or four pages, then click Submit and wait and hope that they will list you.

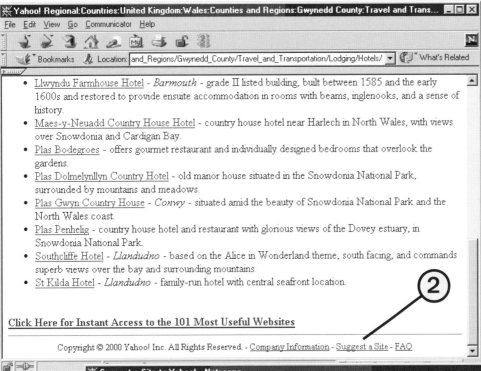

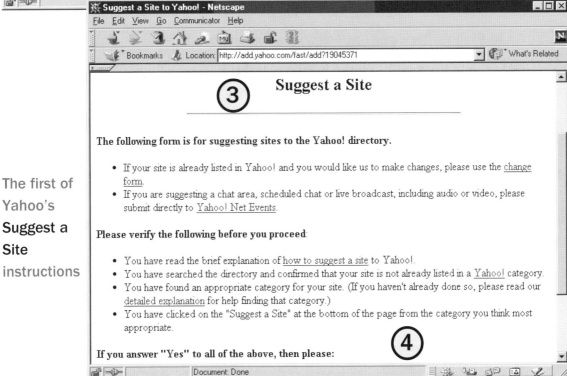

The first of Yahoo's **Suggest a Site** instructions

Search engines

Excite and Alta Vista are the main search engines

Search engines on the other hand use robots, and not humans, to analyse submitted sites. Basically you let them know your URL, and they will eventually get round to 'spidering' your site. The so-called Web spider (get it?) goes to your Web site and logs all the data that it finds onto the search engine's database.

You can easily submit your site to any search engine. Of course, submitting is one thing, getting any prominence on results is another thing. We will address that small problem later!

Excite and AltaVista are the main search engines from the point of view of bringing your site Web traffic in the UK.

Registering with Excite

If you want to get your site listed on Excite, you have to let them know of its existence. Here's how to do that.

1 Go to Excite's front page at http://www.excite.co.uk.

2 Near the bottom of that page is a tiny 'Add URL' link – they try to keep down the numbers submitting by making it difficult to find!

3 Click that link and you are taken to their 'Add URL' page, which is very simple to fill in and submit.

4 You then have to wait till they re-index to see how your submission was received.

AltaVista has a very similar procedure. Again you will find their 'Add an URL' link near the bottom of their front page.

Infoseek, HotBot and a few others have some importance, and you need to be aware that there are hundreds of other search engines with little importance. When you submit your URL to each, it will spider your site. The search engine then analyses your site for inclusion in their database.

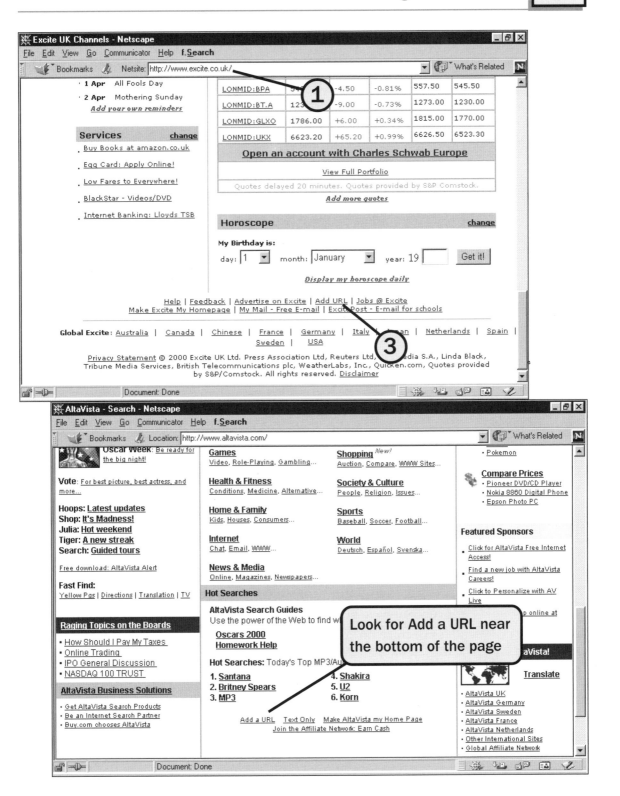

The analysis records all sorts of factors like word density, meta tags (title, keywords, description), coding (of images, headers, links and so on). This information is then stored in the search engine database. When surfers come along ands query the database, they input their query and the search engine uses a mathematical algorithm to rank the pages in its database for relevance to the surfers' queries.

As a Web site owner your problem is that all search engines use different algorithms and even for a particular search engine, the pages returned will vary according to the exact query. For example, if you try three very similar queries on Excite

▷ 'a hotel in the Cotswolds'

▷ 'cotswold hotel'

▷ 'cotswolds hotel'

And you get three very different answers. Who knows how many other ways there are of phrasing this question?

Nobody knows what the algorithm is that Excite uses. If we did know, then every Web site would look identical as designers matched the site to the algorithm.

The problem is further compounded by the fact that it is not just the Web site but other factors, like the number of other Web sites pointing to yours and what their links say, and how popular your site is on that search engine, and how long surfers read your site for. You are not in control of your own destiny here!

You get very different answers on Excite from slightly different queries, and you have no idea which the prospective guest would use. Try the same thing on Alta Vista and you get very different results again. Note that no hotels at all come up when the surfer asks for a 'cotswold hotel'.

You are perhaps now beginning to understand why search engines are a strange black art when it comes to getting your Web site to attract visitors.

Search engines are
a strange black art

Compare the search words and the results
in these two searches at Excite   ▶▶▶

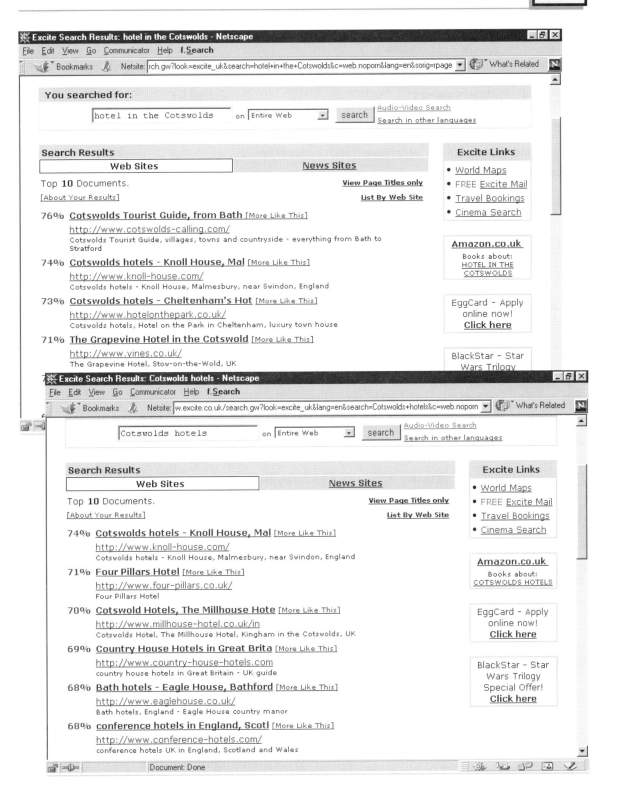

▲
▲
The results of a
search for
'Cotsworld hotel'
at AltaVista

You do not know which engine, nor what search words, they will use. A site that ranks well on one engine may be spurned by another.

On top of that search engines tend to change their algorithms (which they never publish) on a regular basis, and each time you submit a page it may take anything from a few weeks to several months to get added to the database.

So search engine placing is not an exact science but an inexact art. If you are doing your own search engine marketing you need to keep up to date with what is going on in the search engine world by regular visits to sites like **www.searchenginewatch.com** and **searchengineforum.com** which have detailed news on a daily basis.

The top pages at Search Engine Watch
and Search Engine Forums ►►►

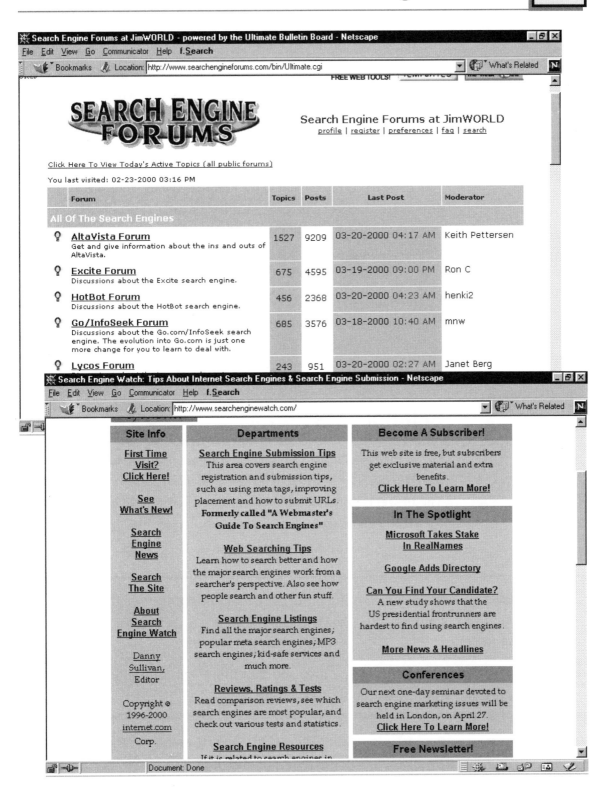

Does search engine positioning matter?

The answer to this question depends on what keywords you have good positioning against, and whether any large numbers of people are actually using that exact choice of keyword.

There are many firms claiming to give you search engine prominence in exchange for a fee. It is unlikely that any of these services will make a more than marginal improvement to the numbers visiting your site, as they are only targeted against a particular word (or words), and only those surfers using those words can find your site. Remember the example above of a surfer wanting a hotel in the Cotswolds, and the variety of queries that they could use to find their business.

▼
▼
▼
▼
▼

Search engine positioning is not as important as most amateurs believe

Undoubtedly good search engine positioning helps, but it is not as important as most amateurs believe. And further it is not the factor that primarilarly dictates the number of visits to your site. Referrals will do more for you in developing the number of visitors to your Web site.

Referral sites

Given that a hotel site can only hope to get so many visits direct from search engines – say five to ten a day – how can it increase this number? The answer is from referral sites – that is from sites that will send (usually for a fee!) visitors from their site to yours. To see how referrals work let us follow a couple of examples.

1 Someone looking for information on Great Britain might try 'Great Britain' with AltaVista, and find http://www.great-britain.co.uk as the first suggestion on their list.

2 While browsing through that site they see that there is information on the Cotswolds on. http://www.cotswolds-calling.com.

A search for 'Great Britain' at AltaVista leads to the Great Britain site, with its regional and other links ▶▶▶

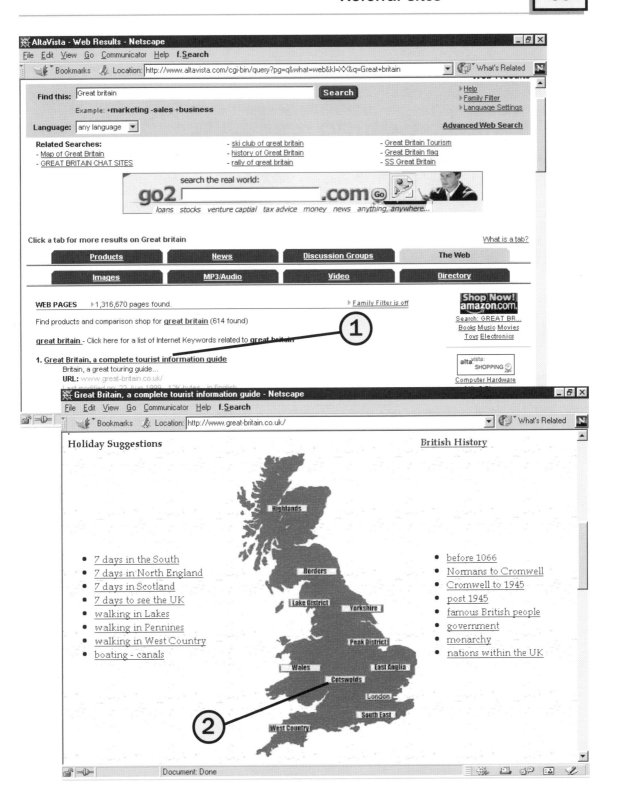

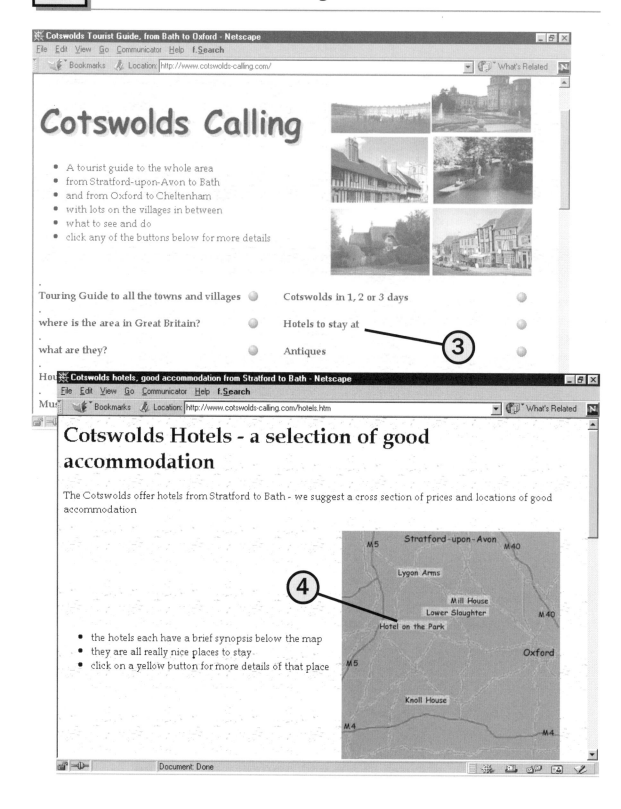

> **3** The Cotswolds link leads them to cotswolds-calling.com.
>
> **4** They look through the information about the Cotswolds and discover a page on hotels in that area, and click on that map for a hotel in Cheltenham.

Finally the surfer has found information about the Hotel on the Park in Cheltenham, but by a circuitous route, not directly from a search engine.

Or someone looking for a country house hotel may try 'country house hotel' in Infoseek and be led to try **http://www.country-house-hotels.com.** Here, a click on 'Wales' will lead to **http://www.country-house-hotels.com/wales.htm** with a map and a choice of country house hotels in Wales. From there, they can reach the site of the hotel that interests them at **http://www.neuadd.com.** This indeed is a country house hotel, but the site has been found by surfing a circuitous route.

Starting to browse for a country house hotel at Infoseek

▼
▼

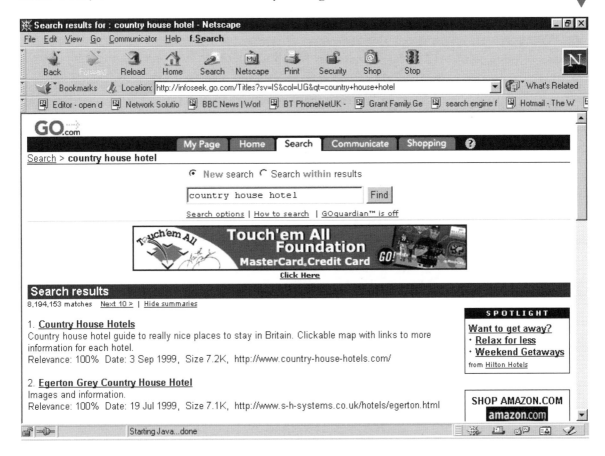

Similarly surfers may find sites like:

    ▷   http://www.smoothhound.co.uk

    ▷   http://www.theaa.co.uk

    ▷   http://www.visitbritain.com

which all offer information on hotels, or

    ▷   http://www.restaurants.co.uk

    ▷   http://www.dine-online.co.uk

which are on-line guides to restaurants in the UK.

How many visitors are you getting?

The Web is a jungle with lots of other Web sites competing for the surfers' attention

How do you find out how many people are looking at your site and who they are ?

The Web is a jungle with lots of other Web sites competing for the surfers' attention, so you have to make sure they find your site. My experience has been that a good hotel site will attract 50 plus visits per day to the site, while the average hotel site attracts just five to ten visits a day.

If your site attracts five visits today, as sure as eggs are eggs, it will get around five tomorrow. No matter that there are 300 million people connected to the Internet, the law of averages dictates that you get just about the same number every day, unless you embark on a long-term strategy to improve your positioning.

In rough terms it needs 100 visits to get a booking, but good site design and a popular destination can improve this conversion of surfers into bookers. Conversely bad design and an unpopular destination will require more visits to get a reservation.

You can only ever get so many visits a day direct from search engines. Even with good search engine positioning, a hotel will only get around ten visits per day direct from search engines. You can expect to get five to ten times this number from good referral sites – that is, sites that send their surfers to your site. So you can generate 50 to 100 visits a day from these referral sites, much more than come direct from search engines.

Yes, yes, but how do you find out about who is looking at your site? The answer to that is in something called your *Log Files*.

Every time a surfer visits you site they leave a trail of information behind. Special software is available to analyse that data. The data is available on the server that houses your Web site. Most free servers will not bother to collect the data, so if you use such free space, the chances are you could never get your hands on the data to analyse it.

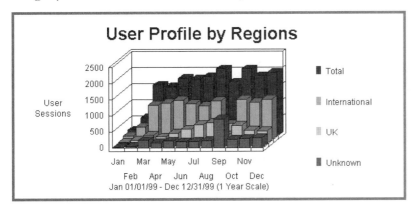

An analysis of visitors to www.neuadd.com

This chart, produced by Web Trends software, shows that around 2000 visits a month were made to the **www.neuadd.com** site in 1999. You need to be careful to separate out in your mind '*hits*' which are meaningless, from '*visits*' which represent individual surfers and means something. Each individual surfer generates around 50 hits, as hit is the techie word for a file, and every little button, every photo, is a separate file. The front page of a Web site may generate 15 hits, and if the surfer looks at two or three pages, then 50 hits will be logged.

Number of user sessions	18871
User sessions from UK	23.11%
International user sessions	61.11%
User sessions of unknown origin	15.77%
Average number of user sessions per day	51
Average user session length	6:05 minutes

Tables also will show which country the surfer came from – treat this cautiously as 'dot com' surfers are analysed as all being from USA, though many are from the UK, e.g. using **aol.com** or **compuserve.com**.

1	United States	10553
2	UK	4362
3	Australia	165
4	Germany	133
5	Canada	77
6	Japan	72
7	Sweden	59
8	Netherlands	45
9	Belgium	44
10	Ireland	39

Another table gives the results of which search engines have been used to find the hotel directly, and which keywords the searchers have used.

1	AltaVista	802	47.68%
2	Yahoo	630	37.45%

And another table tells which site the browser visited before they visited this hotel (this is called the referring site).

1	http://www.neuadd.com/	10174
2	No Referrer	4128
3	http://www.wales-calling.com/	562
4	http://www.altavista.com/	479
5	http://www.wales-snowdonia.com/	473
6	http://www.country-house-hotels.com/	368

The key is knowing whether or not any site offering you a paid link will actually send anyone down that link. The difficulty lies in the fact that big sites may have thousands of surfers a day visiting, but will also have thousands of hotels for the surfer to choose from – the BTA site has over 25,000 choices of accommodation on its database, so it is not surprising that surfers never look at an individual page that often.

The net result is that only a very small number will view any one hotel's page – on average one or two per day would be considered good. And of those looking, only a small percentage will use the paid link to go to your site for more information.

My experience on the AA across a number of hotels is that it averages two per month down a paid link and the BTA less than one per month (these figures are substantially higher only for London).

The smaller specialist sites offering information on a region or type of hotel are more likely to attract quality surfers to your site. A good link site of this sort can deliver many more visits than search engines.

Virtually all other links you may consider are likely to be ineffective. In other words very few people will come down a link that you have swapped with someone, who for example collects Beanie Babies in Wisconsin!

Conclusion

▷　We have seen how to find and register a URL. It is not difficult, nor is it expensive, and a few hours experimenting to find a good URL will repay the time spent.

▷　We have seen how to register your site with search engines and directories. If you focus on the few important directories and engines, you can improve your chances of getting registered on their databases.

▷　And we have seen how to analyse how many visitors a day come to the Web site, and where they have come from – though only if you invest in the analytical software, or if your Web manager provides you with figures.

Armed with this information, you are now in a position to appreciate why design is important. Not just because the surfers are prospective clients, and need to be sold your product, but also because search engines need to database your site in such a way that it will come up in the first few sites when a query is made of that search engine. So on to Web site design…

7

Web site design

▼
▼
▼
▼
▼

A Web site must be designed with two sorts of visitors in mind:

> ▷ **Humans** wanting information on your product;

> ▷ **Robots** visiting your site to harvest information for search engines.

Robot – a program that runs automatically to collect data about Web sites for a search engine.

To accommodate both species, you design your site for the real, human, visitors. When you are happy with the general layout, adapt it as necessary for search engines and their confounded algorithms.

There is little point in having a great Web site unless the maximun number of people can find it. Therefore at least the front page of your Web site must have equal targeting against search engine robots and against the human readers that you hope are going to buy your product.

If you design the site only for humans, it is unlikely ever to come high up on the pages that a search engine will deliver to a surfer requiring information on your area.

This chapter will therefore cover Web design for real readers to appreciate, as well as Web design for search engine spiders to digest.

Designing for humans

After all the site is written for the purpose of selling to the reader. Before you even think about what you want to say, consider the surfers visiting you site, their state of mind and their equipment. They will have already looked at tens if not hundreds of pages, and will only give your page a few seconds' thought before they decide to surf on or stop for a longer look.

Not all surfers have the same equipment many are using:
> ▷ Old, slow modems
> ▷ Bad telephone lines
> ▷ Small screens
> ▷ Different operating systems
> ▷ Different browsers
> ▷ Expensive Internet connection time
> ▷ Aged computers that crash periodically.

First the site has to be quickly found from the server on which it lives. A slow server may take ages between a surfer clicking the link on the search engine where they found you, and actually making contact with the site.

Once found, the site has to download quickly – a good yardstick is not longer than 30 seconds on a 28.8K modem (many of these are still in use). The average Web surfer will just not bother to wait while a screen slowly fills with information. Therefore you have only a few seconds to convince the surfer to stop and delve deeper into your site

Remember that this is a different medium to a printed brochure. Think about all that information on the Web and the ease with which the surfer can move on. A click of a mouse is all that is necessary to leave your site behind forever.

The content of the front page must sell your product with a mixture of punchy photographs and text that shows what you have to offer.

One of my pet hates is a 'click to enter' page. The surfer has to wait ages while the page loads and then wait again before they get information

By and large, for a commercial site like a hotel, the surfer is looking for information, not advertising, and not entertainment. The Internet is about information not advertising.

So how do you design a good front page?

The Web designer must:

▷   Produce the best possible page to sell the product to the surfer in a hurry. One glance is all you are likely to get from the Web site visitor, before they decide to pause to look further, or to surf on.

▷   Maximise the Web site for fast downloading, bearing in mind the 30 seconds on a 28.8K modem test.

▷   Edit the site to allow for the known preferences and eccentricities of search engines.

People judge a site on the first page

The circle is then gone round a second or even a third time to ensure this balance between selling to people and selling to search engine spiders. So first design your front page.

The front page is the most important, as people judge a site on the first page – if they decide to delve further into the site, they will be prepared to wait longer for downloading of inside pages and to wade through detail about particular aspects of your business like the menu in your restaurant or the colour of your wallpaper. If they do not like the front page, they move straight on, and then you have lost them forever.

The front page must have easy links for the browser to navigate to any of the inside pages, without having to read pages in between that are of no interest to them. Too many Web sites try to bully visitors into going from page 1 to page 2, with no option of going to straight to page 7. After a page or two, they will get bored and go off to a more reasonable site.

The front page must allow the visitor to communicate easily with you. Most will want to use e-mail, but some will want to write or phone. So make sure you have an e-mail button, plus address, phone and fax numbers.

▷· It must tell them where you are – it is surprising how many Web sites fail in this aspect. You might know where Shropshire or Snowdonia are, but does someone looking at a computer screen in Illinois know?

▷ Do not include any links to other sites on your front page. Having worked hard to get surfers to look at your site, you do not want them to follow a link somewhere else, and probably never return to your site. If you need or want links, then put them on an inside page, out of harm's way.

So you need to grab visitors with your front page – how do you do this? I usually put on the front page:

▷ Several photographs to show what the hotel is about – outside, inside, all around.

▷ A map indicating where the hotel is located.

▷ A short list of bulleted points to tell the visitor why they should stay at that hotel.

▷ The address, phone number and e-mail address of the hotel.

▷ A navigation bar to other pages on the site. These other pages need be carefully thought out to supply the visitor with the information that they will need.

Overleaf is the full front page for a hotel showing what I mean. It tells the viewer what sort of hotel it is and where it is at a glance. The aim should be to stop in their tracks, those people wanting a really nice country house hotel serving good food.

The page needs to be properly laid out

We come back to the fact that not all surfers are using the same equipment, and in spite of that the design needs to ensure that all people looking at the page see the same thing on their screen, as the original Web designer saw on their screen.

To help lay out a page, a Web designer can use *frames* or *tables*.

The design needs to
ensure that all
people see the
same thing

A good front page will stop surfers in their tracks

▶▶▶▶▶

Hotel

Pen-y-Dyffryn Hotel
Rhydycroesau, Oswestry
Shropshire   SY10 7JD

tel 01691 653700
fax 01691 650066

AA
★★★ ❀ ❀

Good Hotel Guide
Which? Hotel Guide

A Shropshire hotel that is only a hundred yards from Wales.

A hotel in the Shropshire and Wales border hills, this supremely peaceful country house provides the perfect retreat to escape the "madding crowd" and to enjoy this delightful corner of "England-as-it-used-to-be"

- On the Shropshire and Wales border near Oswestry
- Midway between Shrewsbury and Chester
- Built in 1845 of local stone, Pen-y-Dyffryn was constructed as a Georgian Rectory
- Good Hotel Guide and Johansen recommended. Three Star and two Rosettes from the AA.
- Good food and relaxation in an easy-going and sociable atmosphere
- A well stocked bar, wine cellar and crackling log fires
- Those who come simply to unwind will find it hard to do otherwise
- **Click on any of the buttons below for more details**

Hotel   ●

Eating, drinking and relaxing   ●

Things to see and do   ●

Press Reviews and Awards   ●

Maps   ●

Shropshire   ●

Welsh Borders   ●

Prices   ●

e-mail us with reservation or enquiry

e-mail our hotel

Frames versus tables for page layout

What are frames and tables and why do you need to know about them?

A Web page needs to use some method of controlling how it will appear on the viewers' screens. Remember the wide diversity of computers, screens, modems, operating systems, out there in cyberspace. You would like to be reasonably sure that, for example, three photographs with captions underneath, will appear in the same position on the viewers' screens and that the caption under each remains in the correct place when viewed on another screen on the other side of the world.

The two ways of doing this are to use frames or tables. Look on them as part of the armoury of programming tools available to a Web designer.

Frames are independent subsections of pages. For example, a page may have two frames, perhaps one with a navigation bar, the rest with information. The navigation bar can be left constant, and only the information frame changed when the viewer goes on to the next page.

The big drawback to frames is that they are not handled well by search engines and you lose control over how the search engine will index your site. The bottom line is *do not use frames*. Very few Web sites do now and search engine difficulties are the main reason.

The bottom line is, do not use frames

That leaves you with tables to lay out your page design.

Let us try to show you what tables actually are, as you will not always see them when you surf the Internet. They can have highly visible coloured borders and dividers, or be used as part of the background coding to control the layout of your page, but with the borders turned off so that they are not themselves seen. A table really just puts a grid onto the page, and the designer can then drop photographs or text into boxes on it.

So you can see how the table layout (given by the dotted lines on the Web page in the example overleaf) enables the programmer to set the pictures and the copy in the right place, and that all viewers will (as much as possible) see it in the same way. For example the caption '**weddings**' will always go under the Weddings button, and so on.

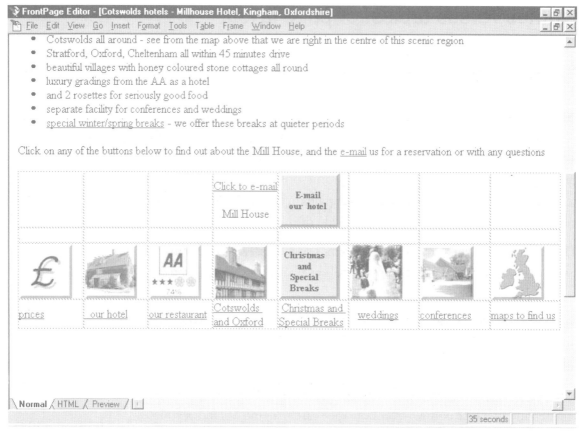

▲

Here, I have let the coding show through – visitors do not normally see the outline of tables

The big drawback to tables is that most browsers will not display any of a table's content until it all has been downloaded. If you have a lot of graphics in a table, this can give the surfer a long wait before anything is visible – not a good idea. The problem is, of course, much worse if everything on the page is built into one big table.

Tables are best used within pages, and preferably after initial headings and/or text so that the viewer has something to read while the table contents download. They are also best kept small. You can use several together if you need to arrange a large quanitity of material, that way the first parts will be visible while the rest comes in.

Using graphics on a Web page

Remember the Internet is not a printed medium. You can put onto a Web site as many photographs or other graphics as you want, in order to convey the information you need to your prospective clients.

No hotel brochure could have photos of every bedroom, plus the view from the bedroom window – but your Web site could do that if you wanted. No hotel brochure could give details of a selection of local walks complete with a dozen photos along the way on each – a Web site can.

How do you acquire graphics?

Clip art is widely available. You can buy CDs full of clip art, and many Microsoft applications include the Clip Gallery. There are hundreds, sometimes millions of clip art items available on this and similar software packages. All you do is scroll through the myriad of clip art examples, and just insert whichever ones take your fancy into your Web site.

A selection from Microsoft's Clip Gallery

Avoid irritating your visitors! The rotating e-mail sign or the bounding Scottie dog are fine if you have never seen them before, but grate if they are on 10% of pages on the Internet

For *logo design*, you can use other programs, like WordArt, and create logos of different shapes and colours

WordArt Gallery is part of the Microsoft Word and Works packages

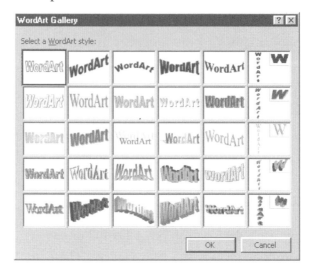

If you want some help with logo design, try one of the good free sites on the Web, like CoolText.com, that show you how to produce a top class design from the template.

To make a Web site work, you will need lots of *photographs*.

If you are really serious about having a Web site, then you will need a digital camera. This enables you to take masses of photographs, download them straight onto your computer, edit them to the size and shape you want, and put them onto your Web site. All this without the need for developing or scanning photos.

Alternatively you need to have a scanner and scan photographs into your computer, then edit them from there. The problem you may have, is that if you use other people's photgraphs, then they may/will take great exception to your using them – a breach of copyright laws tends to be more apparent on a Web site then on a printed brochure with limited distribution.

Photographs for Web sites do not have to be of professional quality as you will undoubtedly have to take out a lot of the detail in order to make them download quickly enough.

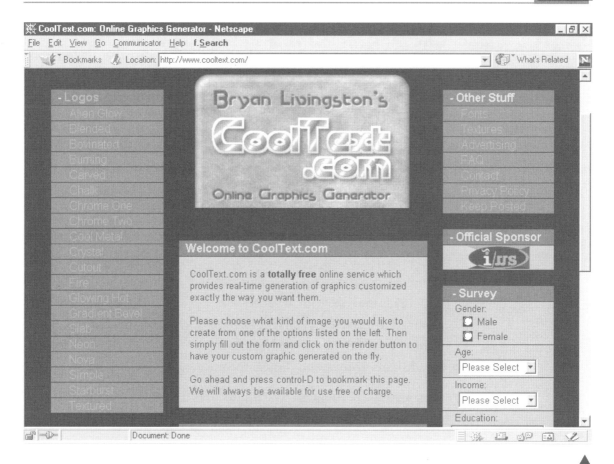

After the great design, what next?

▲
▲
Try CoolText.com for
logos and graphics

The answer to this question is to make the site download quicker. This is to get the information on your Web site from cyberspace into your Web visitor's browser as quickly as possible.

You need to make sure that your Web site adheres to the rule of completing a download in under 30 seconds, over a 28.8K modem. It is the amount of information being transferred that dictates download time. When you are talking about things like file size, information is normally measured in bytes, with a thousand bytes to a kilobyte, or Kb. For reasons best known to the techies, modem speeds are measured in kilobits – and eight bits make one byte. And when data is being sent down the line, it is packaged up with error-checking and flow control stuff that adds slightly to the overall quantity of data.

▼
▼
▼
▼
▼
To download in
under 30 seconds,
you shouldn't have
more than 60Kb of
files on the page

What this means in practice is that a 28.8K modem will actually transfer under 3Kb of data every second – and that assumes that there are no hold-ups anywhere else between your visitor and your site. It is safer to work on the basis that files will be transferred at under 2Kb per second. So, to complete a download in under 30 seconds, you shouldn't have more than around 60Kb of files on the page.

Written copy does not take up many bytes and contributes very little to the length required to download a Web page. Pictures contain large amounts of data, and need to be adapted to carry less information and hence download faster. What this really amounts to is making photographs fuzzier, as less detail means removing information from them.

GIF (Graphics Interchange Format) – a compact graphic format, very suitable for simple images with a limited colour range.

JPG or JPEG (Joint Photographic Experts Group) – a compressed file format for photographs and high-colour images. A range of compression levels are available, and the higher the compression, the smaller the file but also the greater the loss of detail.

Normally two sorts of picture files are used: *JPEG* for photographs, and *GIF* for illustrations with fewer colours. Both picture formats have bytes removed to make them smaller without losing too much detail. These formats can both be handled by browsers. Any other graphics formats require extra software to display the images.

I use a software program which puts photos side by side so that I can reduce the detail until I have a balance between detail and download time.

The screen on page 119 shows three images side by side:

▷　The left image is the original and has a file size of 36Kb

▷　The central image has only 60% of the detail and a file size of 16Kb

▷　The right image is down to 20% of the detail and a file size of 8Kb.

What it means to the surfer is that the lefthand image takes 20 seconds to download, but the righthand one only takes 5 seconds. You can see that if you have three such photos on a page, then it is the difference between surfers getting the page in 15 seconds or having to wait 60 seconds, which is too long, and they will undoubtedly decide to surf on rather than wait.

You must remember that the surfer has many options open to them other than your site, so they won't wait while your razor-sharp photo downloads. Inside pages can have more detailed photographs, as the surfer has by then decided to stay and actually requires more detailed information.

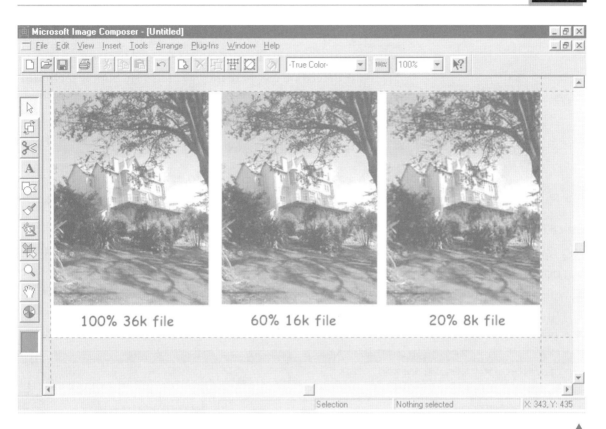

Designing the inside pages

Plan the site around page headings on which you believe the Web visitor would like to have information about your business.

▷ Every page must have an e-mail button so that the user can easily contact you for more information or make a booking.

▷ Every page must carry navigation buttons, so that the visitor does not get lost – if they do, they are likely to hit the 'eject' button to escape. After that you have lost them.

The pages depend on your business and what you are particularly proud of. A selection of items for a hotel might be:

▷ **Prices** – the surfer certainly wants to know what the product costs, and this information needs to be correct and up to date. The prices page is the one that is most often visited after the front page.

Finding the balance between image size and quality using Image Composer

The prices page is the one that is most often visited

▷ **Where you are**. While you hopefully know where you are, the average surfer may well not know where Aberavon, Avon or Angus are in relation to where they want to visit. Supply them with a series of maps from UK level down to street level.

▷ **A tour of your hotel**. Remember this is a different medium, so a scanned-in hotel brochure will not do.

People read a screen in a different way to a sheet of paper. They scan rather than read, and pictures are easier and cheaper to use on the Internet than in print.

QuickTime movies can give 360° views but add greatly to download time

▼
▼

This means each page needs a punchy layout, so that the reader can take it all in as they scan the page. Remember that photographs put points across particularly well on the computer screen.

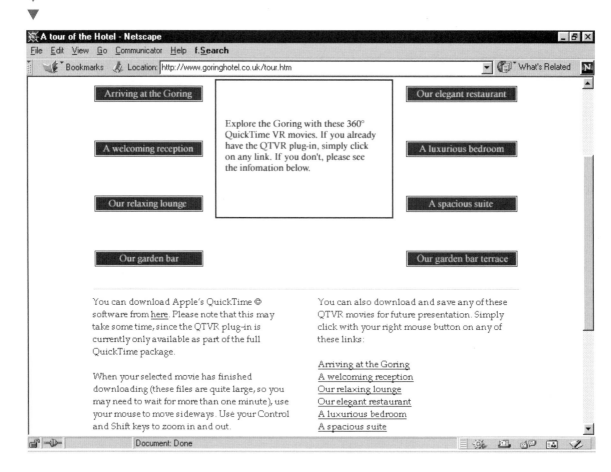

Multimedia

Do not go over the top with multimedia, that is special effect like 360 degree cameras, moving images (flash) or sound.

Remember the surfer does not want to be entertained, they want information. And they will move on if your Web site presents too many difficulties.

▷ You can have special software that will give all-round vision, the Goring Hotel has got a nice gizmo that gives 360 degree vision for internal photgraphs, but to get the benefit of this technology the surfer has to download special software and install that software before they can view the effect.

You can see the dilemma the surfer faces, do they spend time downloading software to look at the 360 degree vision, or do they ignore it?

In the case of the Goring Hotel this information is on an inside page, so the surfer has already embarked on exploring the site.

Music

Some Web sites add music – research has shown that a number of problems exist with music. My advice is to avoid it, because:

▷ It takes time for the music file to transfer to the surfer's computer. It all adds to the waiting for something to happen time.

▷ Music is protected by copyright, and record companies are becoming very vigilant at protecting their copyright. If you want to use someone else's music on your site, you must have their permission.

▷ Users of the Internet tend to dislike music appearing in their living room or office desk.

▷ The short excerpts that sites have are not particularly mood setting.

My advice is to avoid music

Web site design

Shockwave Flash

If you use
Shockwave Flash,
you must provide a
plain alternative –
and make it easy to
find!

▼

▼

This is an interesting technology that enables a Web site to show moving graphics, without excessively long delays. However, before you can view the site, you have to download the special software – it's free, but it takes time to get it from cyberspace, and install on your computer.

This Italian hotel has had to put a warning on its front page for visitors to read before entering the site. If you read the small print, you will see that you can get the information without Shockwave Flash, but how many surfers are going to hang around to read that small print?

The average surfer wants information quickly. You have to weigh up the advantages of perhaps getting more information across with 360 degree cameras, or to portray your mood with music or entertain with Shockwave

Flash— against the disadvantage of the user needing special software or the site taking longer to download.

Apart from that, gizmos cost you money!

Adapt your design for the search engines

So having got your Web site designed to your, and hopefully your prospective client's, satisfaction, the next problem is to adapt it so that search engines will place it high on their list of suggestions when a user interrogates their database.

Search engines do not 'read' your site in the sense of understanding what it says. They hoover up all the information on your site from the HTML coding. Anyone can see this coding, just open the **View** menu on your

The HTML code that creates a Web page

```
Source of: http://www.bathqueensberry.com/fintro.html - Netscape

<HTML>

        <HEAD>
<title>hotel Bath England - AA 3 Red Stars - The Queensberry Hotel</title>

<meta name="keywords" content="Bath, hotels, BATH, HOTELS, Hotels, hotel, England, Britain, accor

<meta name="description" content="hotel Bath England - The Queensberry - AA 3 Red Stars - private
</HEAD>
<NOFRAMES><!--hotels Bath England - AA 3 red stars - The Queensberry - privately owned Georgian
<!--hotels Bath England, hotel, bath, Britain, b&b, bed and breakfast, Queensberry, Queensbury,
</NOFRAMES>


<FRAMESET ROWS="95,235,*" FRAMEBORDER="0" BORDER="0" FRAMESPACING="0">
        <FRAME SRC="butcode/bintro.html" NAME="head" SCROLLING="NO" FRAMEBORDER="0" >
        <FRAME SRC="intro.html" NAME="text" SCROLLING="NO" FRAMEBORDER="0" >
        <FRAME SRC="sintro.html" NAME="strap" SCROLLING="NO" FRAMEBORDER="0" >
</FRAMESET>
<BODY TOPMARGIN=8 LEFTMARGIN=8 BGCOLOR="#FFFFFF" LINK="#ffffff" ALINK="#ffffff" VLINK="#ffffff"
<TABLE BORDER=0 CELLSPACING=0 CELLPADDING=0 WIDTH="99%">
<TR VALIGN=TOP>
<TD WIDTH=580><B><FONT COLOR="#FFFFFF">hotel Bath England - AA 3 red star The Queensberry Hotel,
<TR VALIGN=TOP>
<TD WIDTH=580><B><FONT COLOR="#FFFFFF">hotels Bath England - all bedrooms with private bath, TV
<TR VALIGN=TOP>
<TD WIDTH=580><B><FONT COLOR="#FFFFFF">Bath hotels England - all bedrooms with private bath, TV
<TR VALIGN=TOP>
<TD WIDTH=580><B><FONT COLOR="#FFFFFF">hotel Bath England - all bedrooms with private bath, TV a
<TR VALIGN=TOP>
<TD WIDTH=580><B><FONT COLOR="#FFFFFF">HOTELS BATH ENGLAND - all bedrooms with private bath, TV
```

browser, when you have the page you want to examine in your browser window, and then select **Page Source** from the options on offer. The screenshot on the previous page shows a typical page source. It may be Double Dutch to you, but it gives a wealth of information to a search engine.

There are several things that search engines consider important when ranking your site.

Consider this example of someone wanting a hotel in Kent, and going to AltaVista. You can see from the screen below that there are over 6 million references that AltaVista has covering this query. How do you make sure that you come out top of the pile when this happens? What is the secret that Rowhill Grange Hotel has that all the other hotels in Kent do not

How do you get to be number 1?

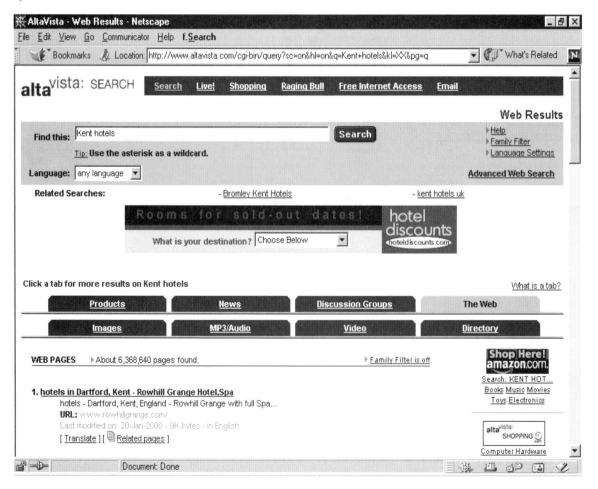

have, to make AltaVista recommend it as the most relevant Web site to match the query?

Research and common sense tell us that the average Web user does not go beyond the first 25 suggestions on the list that a search engine serves up against any given query.

Well the answer lies in how AltaVista, or any other search engine indexes the site. The sort of information that it will store includes:

▷ The URL

▷ The *title* tag

▷ The *meta* tags for *description* and *keywords*. Meta tags are the programmer's opportunity to tell the robot what the Web site wants recorded – if you have no meta tags you lose out. See the screen showing source code to see where meta tags are found.

▷ The text, including the order of the words. Words appearing at the start of sentences are ranked more highly than words at the end of sentences. Also the spread of words across a page – if a keyword appears at the start of the page and at the end of the page, it is considered that that keyword is important for that page.

▷ The *alt* tags – the text that is displayed if images are not loaded.

▷ The *header* tags – the text in headlines.

▷ Link text (the wording that is highlighted in links) and the link destinations (that is the names of the places that the links lead to).

So much for the information stored from your site. To answer a question about 'Kent hotels', the search engine then uses a mathematical algorithm to give a weighting to other factors, such as:

▷ The number of links pointing to your site from other Web sites.

▷ The relevance of those links – in other words whether the remote links are using your keywords.

▷ Whether the remote sites linking to you are themselves related to your keywords.

▷   The popularity of your site on that search engine – how many people are accessing it.

▷   The length of time surfers spend looking at your site when they access it.

Apart from giving your Web sites points for the various factors outlined above, the algorithm may well subtract points for what is known in the trade as '*spamming*' – where the site author tries to load the site in a way that gets it unfair prominence.

Most search engines have got wise to spamming

Spamming is a series of tricks that most search engines have got wise to. For example, they will penalise you if you:

▷   Put keywords in the page too many times in whatever way – for example, written many times in the keywords meta tag or repeatedly mentioned in the main copy.

▷   Try to add keyword heavy text in the same colour as the background – so that the human reader cannot see it, but the robots can.

▷   Try to create multiple front pages with different keywords.

▷   Register lots of URLs and have them point to your original URL.

In the case of this example there are over 6 million Web pages on the AltaVista database with the keywords 'Kent' or 'hotels'. The AltaVista computer has then examined all of these in microseconds and used its mathematical algorithm to produce its recommendation for the most relevant hotels for the search engine user. Up has come the answer that 'Rowhill Grange' is, in the opinion of AltaVista, the most relevant.

Life can be very unfair for the Web designer

If you go to Excite or Yahoo you may well get a different answer. And if you try altering your site to come top on Excite, it may well slip down the ratings on AltaVista. Life can be very unfair for the Web designer.

The next step, you might think, would be to submit different pages for AltaVista and Excite, but the catch is that the search engines give more relevance to the page with a file name 'index.htm' which is automatically your front page, so multiple pages cannot all have this name, and so they get less relevance.

Take it from me:

▷ Your site can never be top of all search engines for a particular keyword, and even if it was, it would not matter as there would be a variey of ways of submitting the query and the site would never be top on all permutions of querying those keywords.

▷ There is no magic potion that guarantees you better placing. Any tricks have been found by people in the past and the search engines have already plugged the gap, and are now penalising sites that are still using these technniques.

▷ As long as you have reasonable search engine prominence and keep monitoring it, so that your site does not suddenly get electronically washed off a database for no good reason, then that is the best you can do.

▷ Remember it is not your own favourite search engine that matters, it is the ones that the bulk of people are using. Currently most visitors will come from Yahoo, Excite, AltaVista and InfoSeek.

▷ And bear in mind that, whatever happens, real people reading your site must be convinced to buy your product.

Conclusion

▷ Grab people's attention by having a fast downloading site with easy to digest selling points.

▷ Be clear on the information that you want to give on inside pages and produce a section for each of these themes.

▷ Offer easy navigation for the surfer through the Web site. Ensure they know where they are on the site and can find their way to any other page, and that every page is easily accessible.

▷ Put an easy, foolproof way of contacting you by e-mail on every page.

▷   Ensure the surfer knows how to contact you by phone or post as well.

▷   Be clear and single-minded on what keywords you wish to target your site against.

▷   Maximise your site's profile against your chosen keywords on all points of programming.

▷   Keep up to date with search engine news.

▷   Do not try to fool search engines, they will not like it and will penalise you.

In the end, content is king

▷   In the end *content is king*. Get your content right and the search engine positioning will follow – not the other way round.

8

Building your own site

The objective of this chapter is to give you a simple grounding in how to write and publish your own Web site. It does not set out to be a fully comprehensive guide – you would need a full text book to achieve that goal – but is designed to show you how it can be done by someone who is not a professional computer programmer.

You will not need to acquire any detailed programming knowledge, but you will need to understand something about the background to the process before you start.

Let us a look first at the pros and cons of writing your own site.

▷ It is the cheapest way of getting a site. It can be done for anything from nothing to a few hundred pounds – more on cost later.

▷ You are in control, so you can make as many changes or additions as you want.

▷ It can be fun – in a masochistic sort of way – if you enjoy playing with computers.

However

▷ Writing the site is really less than half the problem. The more important part is getting people to look at your new Web site.

▷ Web marketing and good search engine placement is much more difficult.

So only write the site if you are prepared to go on and ensure that surfers can and do find your Web site among the millions already out there in cyberspace.

You need to understand something about the background before you start

Background to Web page coding

Every Web page uses a common coding system called HTML – Hyper Text Markup Language – which makes it possible for all those different computers across the world to read each other's Web sites.

There are PCs and Apples, there are mainframe computers and laptops, there are chip manufacturers other than Intel, there are operating systems other than Windows, there are different sized screens and different browsers. A fairly basic common coding language needs to be used to enable anyone, with any combination of hardware and software to read a Web site. HTML is that language.

To create your own site you can either learn to write in HTML, or buy software that will enable you to create it without having to use HTML.

DIY HTML

Learn to write in HTML and upload your site to a bit of cyberspace using an FTP (File Transfer Protocol) program – this is the option for those with a lot of time and very little money, who on top of that will want to use the experience gained to go on and write more Web sites. Unless you are very short of money and are actually interested in programming, then avoid this option!

WS_FTP is used to upload files to your ISP's server – you can get a copy from www.ipswitch.com

▼
▼

You can write the pages for the Web site in Notepad (one of the Windows Accessories) and load it to your Web space with an FTP program. The best of these is WS_FTP, which you can download from the Internet site www.ipswitch.com.

There may be a high degree of satisfaction when, and if, you finally get your Web site up and running, but for the average business, the cost savings just do not warrant the time spent on learning how to do it.

Use an HTML editor like FrontPage

Read more about
FrontPage at
Microsoft's site

FrontPage makes the whole process no more complicated that learning a new word-processing program. It avoids you having to know anything about the actual coding, and enables you to concentrate on designing your Web site. FrontPage is what is known in the trade as a WYSIWYG

editor (What You See Is What You Get) – in other words, you see the words and images laid out just as the surfer will see them, and not the HTML coding that lies beneath.

There are a number of such HTML editors on the market. The purpose of this chapter is not to contrast and compare each and every Web publishing program. Instead we take you through the writing, publishing and maintaining your own Web site using Front Page so that you can see the basics of how to do it yourself.

FrontPage is no more difficult to learn, than it is to learn to use a word processing package. You may find that statement good news, or you may find it bad news.

FrontPage and FrontPage Express

There are two versions of FrontPage.

▷ FrontPage 2000 is the full-feature version, selling at around £160 or as part of the Office 2000 suite. It contains some very comprehensive site-management software to keep track of your files, plus other utilities as well as the HTML editor.

▷ FrontPage Express is the cut-down version, containing only the HTML editor. It is free with Internet Explorer.

If you are aiming to build a relatively simple site with perhaps half a dozen or so pages, then FrontPage Express will probably be all you need. Once you start to get beyond this, the extra facilities and efficiency of the full FrontPage will start to justify its cost.

The road to publishing your own Web site

If you are doing it yourself, you need to go through the following steps:

1: **Register your own URL.** As explained in Chapter 6, this is not a requirement, but if you do not have your own URL, then the chances are that fewer visitors will end up looking at your Web site.

2: **Find somewhere to park your Web site.** A site has to live on a computer that is permanently connected to the Internet, and that is capable of sending your pages to surfers anxious to see them.

3: **Design and write the Web site.**

4: **Publish it** by uploading it to your reserved corner of cyberspace.

5: **Register it with search engines** and market it in a way that the maximum number of people can find it.

6: **Update it**, and modify it as necessary on a day-to-day basis.

1: Register your own URL

Chapter 6 told you how to check the availability of 'dot com' and 'dot co dot uk' Web names. If you checked you will see that in fact, at that point in the book, you did not have all the data to fill up the online registration form. You were missing details of where your URL was going to be parked – technical stuff about things called '*name servers*'. Once you get your own Web space, you can fill in those blanks. The person you buy your Web space from will give you the technical details necessary for completing registration, or else will register it for you for a modest fee.

2: Procure Web space

You need to place your Web site on a server that is permanently connected to the Internet. A little research will show you that you have two options – either using free Web space, or buying commercial space.

Free Web space

As someone once said, there is no such thing as a free lunch. Consider why anyone would want to offer you free Web space?

Why would anyone want to offer you free Web space?

To sell you something else, for example, sell you an Internet connection service like Global. They offer an Internet connection for so much a year, and thrown in with that, they hold out the carrot of a chunk of free Web space for you to use.

As you have already bought something from them, they will offer some free technical support, but there will be limits on what they will do for you. They will probably point you to their Web page called FAQ, which has detailed answers to common questions, and may offer an on-line tutorial to guide you through the process of creating pages and setting up your site on their server.

Also you cannot normally use your own URL with these free Web space deals you will have a Web address like:

http://www.users.globalnet.co.uk/~grandhotel

Where '**grandhotel**' is the only choice you have in the name – you are stuck with the rest of the URL.

Like Global, most ISPs are happy to give you the Web space, but are not prepared to spend much time or money on teaching you to use it.

Global offer some guidance on creating and publishing Web pages

▼
▼

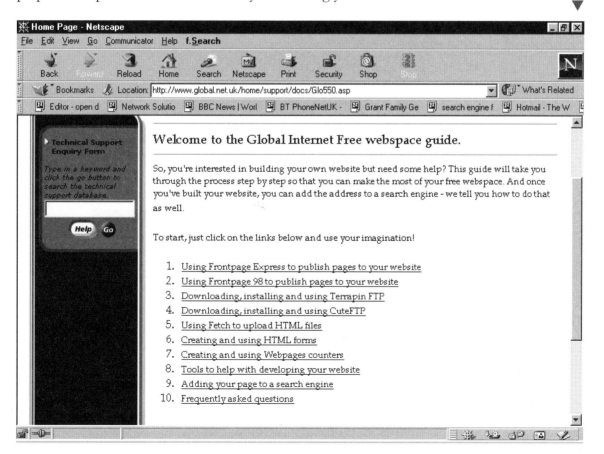

Welcome to the Global Internet Free webspace guide.

So, you're interested in building your own website but need some help? This guide will take you through the process step by step so that you can make the most of your free webspace. And once you've built your website, you can add the address to a search engine - we tell you how to do that as well.

To start, just click on the links below and use your imagination!

1. Using Frontpage Express to publish pages to your website
2. Using Frontpage 98 to publish pages to your website
3. Downloading, installing and using Terrapin FTP
4. Downloading, installing and using CuteFTP
5. Using Fetch to upload HTML files
6. Creating and using HTML forms
7. Creating and using Webpages counters
8. Tools to help with developing your website
9. Adding your page to a search engine
10. Frequently asked questions

Freeserve provides
some online help,
but if you need
technical support, it
will cost you
▼
▼

They may also give you free Web space so as to make money from you indirectly (a cut of your phone bill perhaps) or like Freeserve.

You do not have to pay Freeserve anything for an Internet connection, and they will give you free Web space for your site as well. As with Global, you have to accept the Web address they give you, which is something like **www.grandhotel.freeserve.co.uk**. This tends to look a bit cheap if you use it for a business site and have to print that as your Web address.

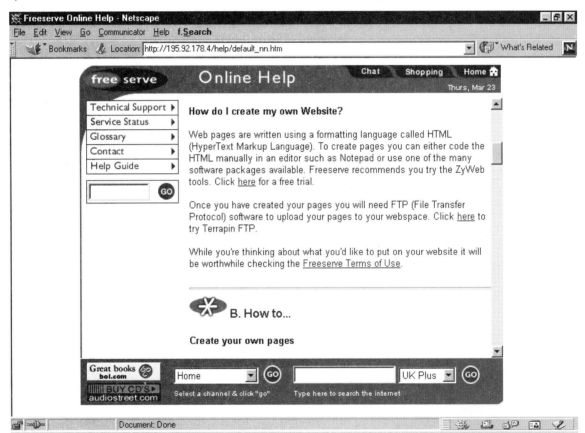

The other price you pay with many of the 'free' sites, is the cost of technical support. You have to pay if you need help in using the free space, if for example you cannot make the thing work, can only get one page published or cannot get a password to take. It is free only as long as you can solve any problem yourself, otherwise you will have to pay from 50p to £1.00 a minute if you need to phone them, and that includes time spent in a telephone queue with muzak playing.

Commercial Web space

For a business site you are always better buying you own Web space. The advantages are:

▷ You can use your own URL, such as **www.grandhotel.co.uk**.

▷ You get technical support without paying for it by the minute.

▷ You ought to get the benefit of a faster, more reliable server – that is, surfers should be able to download your site faster, whatever speed of modem they themselves are using, and the site should be always available for surfers to visit.

▷ As you have paid for the service, if you have any problem then you can get it put right. With a free service, you really have no rights if your Web site is down, slow or otherwise disadvantaged.

it is worth your while paying the small sum for these advantages

You discover as time goes by that it is worth your while paying the small sum necessary for these advantages.

So how do you go about finding a company that will sell you Web space? There are a number of methods – here are two simple but effective approaches.

Go to a directory like Yahoo and wend your way to **Regional > Countries > United Kingdom > Business and Economy > Companies > Internet Services > Web Services** to find a list of companies offering a variety of Web services. You will find a good cross-section and brief write up on each. Not all are necessarily offering what we are looking for – Web hosting – but the descriptions make it fairly clear which do.

It is worthwhile looking up a few of their clients, and perhaps contacting the clients by e-mail, asking if they can recommend that supplier. Existing clients may have suffered problems, for example, the ISP may not offer technical support at the weekends or over public holidays, or their servers may be slow or unreliable.

Remember the Internet is a 24 hour a day marketing medium and you cannot afford to be off-line for significant periods of time.

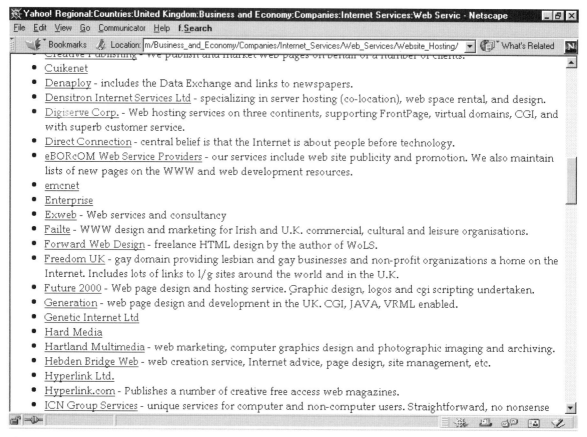

Yahoo! Regional:Countries:United Kingdom:Business and Economy:Companies:Internet Services:Web Servic - Netscape

File Edit View Go Communicator Help f.**Search**

Bookmarks Location: m/Business_and_Economy/Companies/Internet_Services/Web_Services/Website_Hosting/ ▼ What's Related N

- Creative Publishing - we publish and market web pages on behalf of a number of clients.
- Cuikenet
- Denaploy - includes the Data Exchange and links to newspapers.
- Densitron Internet Services Ltd - specializing in server hosting (co-location), web space rental, and design.
- Digiserve Corp. - Web hosting services on three continents, supporting FrontPage, virtual domains, CGI, and with superb customer service.
- Direct Connection - central belief is that the Internet is about people before technology.
- eBORcOM Web Service Providers - our services include web site publicity and promotion. We also maintain lists of new pages on the WWW and web development resources.
- emcnet
- Enterprise
- Exweb - Web services and consultancy
- Failte - WWW design and marketing for Irish and U.K. commercial, cultural and leisure organisations.
- Forward Web Design - freelance HTML design by the author of WoLS.
- Freedom UK - gay domain providing lesbian and gay businesses and non-profit organizations a home on the Internet. Includes lots of links to l/g sites around the world and in the U.K.
- Future 2000 - Web page design and hosting service. Graphic design, logos and cgi scripting undertaken.
- Generation - web page design and development in the UK. CGI, JAVA, VRML enabled.
- Genetic Internet Ltd
- Hard Media
- Hartland Multimedia - web marketing, computer graphics design and photographic imaging and archiving.
- Hebden Bridge Web - web creation service, Internet advice, page design, site management, etc.
- Hyperlink Ltd.
- Hyperlink.com - Publishes a number of creative free access web magazines.
- ICN Group Services - unique services for computer and non-computer users. Straightforward, no nonsense

Yahoo has a very comprehensive list of Web service companies

Purchase one of the Internet magazines available in any newsagents. Go through the adverts in those magazines and again try to check out any you are interested in by looking at their site and their clients on-line

I have had my own sites parked with Digiserve for two years, and found their service very good. Take a look round their site. As with all purveyors of Web space, you will find a guide as to exactly what they offer and you can fill up a form on-line and pay via credit card for the service. The Web space will then be made available to you within a few hours.

Once signed up, and with your credit card checked out, they will allocate to you a unique Web address, as in the example we used in Chapter 6 of '195.172.86.102' for **www.stmartinshotel.co.uk**. They are supplying you with space at '195.172.86.102'. They let the computers at the 'dot co dot uk' people know that **www.stmartinshotel.co.uk** is available at this number, and if you have done your paperwork correctly this information

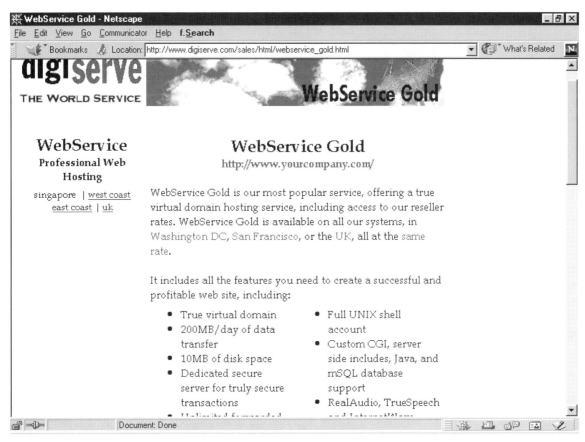

is then made available to all Web users, who will find the site when they type **www.stmartinshotel.co.uk** into their browsers. It takes from initially purchasing the Web space, around 24 hours for everyone on the Internet to get your site in this way.

Setting up your own Web server

In theory, you could cut out the middleman completely and set up your own Web server, but in practice this is not a serious option for any but the largest hotels. You would need a dedicated computer, but this is not the main cost – a suitable computer with all the necessary software can now (mid-2000) be had for less than £1,000. The big costs are in maintaining a permanent connection to the Internet, 24 hours a day, and you need a competent computer professional working at least part-time. A big hotel or a chain that already has a substantial computer installation might well think about running their own server, but not otherwise.

Digiserve, like most Web hosts, offers several levels of service

3: Design and write your site

The advice at the start of this chapter was not to try creating sites using raw coding and an FTP program, but to use an HTML editor and site management package like Microsoft's FrontPage, the market leader in this area. FrontPage comes on a CD and is simple to install on your PC.

You are now ready to write your first Web site. In this section we will take you through the steps of getting your Web site running using FrontPage.

First design your Web site as discussed in Chapter 7. It is important to think out exactly how you want your business portrayed to the world.

▷ The front page is the most important. If it is not designed with search engines in mind, then few surfers will ever find your site via search engines, but if human visitors do not like what they find on your front page, they will surf straight on.

▷ The inside pages of the Web site must carry the details of your business in such a way that you can present to prospective customers the pertinent details of your business.

It will help if you sketch out the front page of the Web site on paper first, so that you know what you are trying to achieve.

You are now ready to let FrontPage step you through the process of making a Web site.

It will help if you sketch out the front page on paper first

---

1 At the Getting Started dialog box, click on Create a New FrontPage Web, then click OK.

2 This leads you to another dialog box to create your new Web. Here you should select Empty Web – if you want to build one from scratch, as we do – and give it a title, e.g. 'Grand-Hotel', then click OK.

3 After that you just do as the instruction says – To create a Home Page, click New Page on the toolbar. Do that and FrontPage spoons up a blank page in the FrontPage Editor, on which you can write your masterpiece.

4 Type in your text and insert clip art or photographs.

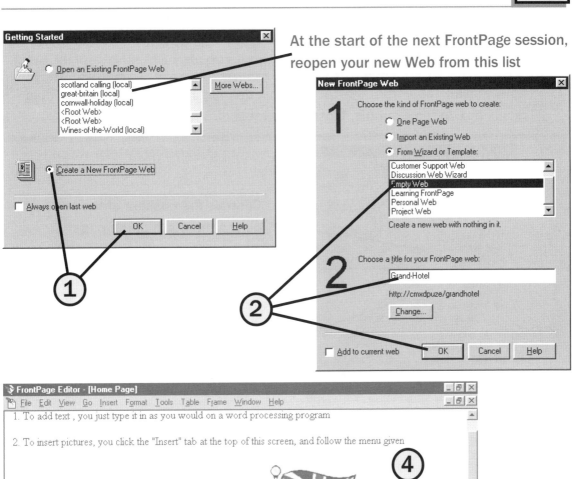

At the start of the next FrontPage session, reopen your new Web from this list

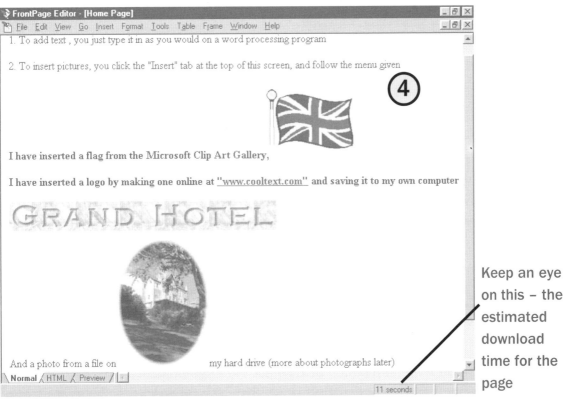

Keep an eye on this – the estimated download time for the page

So you have a page and have added a photograph and clip art to it. How do you make it look better? Answer, use a table to control the layout.

5 Select Insert Table from the Table menu, defining its size at the Insert Table dialog box. In the example, I inserted a table of 3 rows and 3 columns.

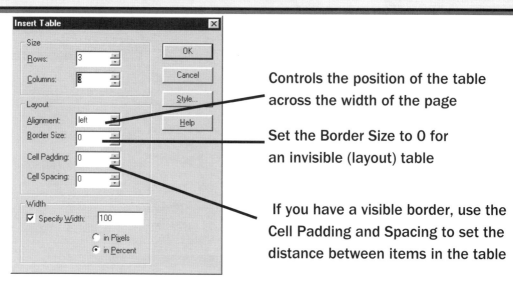

Controls the position of the table across the width of the page

Set the Border Size to 0 for an invisible (layout) table

If you have a visible border, use the Cell Padding and Spacing to set the distance between items in the table

I then dropped my illustrations into it, then put in a name and address and added a button from clip art for e-mail, and finally gave it a background using the tools available on FrontPage.

The next stage is to create the inside pages. At first these are all blank, but it gives you a structure and you can start to make links between the pages.

6 Switch to FrontPage Explorer and click the New Page button once for each page. Give them appropriate names, such as 'prices', 'maps', 'restaurant'.

Once you have added these empty pages, all you have to do is create a '*hyperlink*' to each from the front page. A hyperlink is a piece of text or an image that the surfer clicks on to get taken to the linked page.

7 Type and select the text to be linked, e.g. the word '*Prices*' to link to the prices page, then open the Insert menu and select Hyperlink.

8 At the Create Hyperlink dialog box, select the page and click OK.

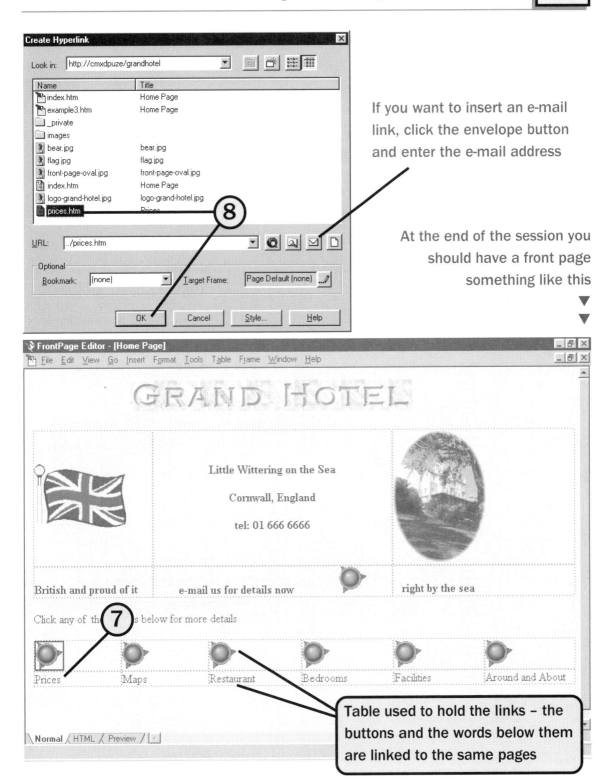

If you want to insert an e-mail link, click the envelope button and enter the e-mail address

At the end of the session you should have a front page something like this

Table used to hold the links – the buttons and the words below them are linked to the same pages

You now have all the necessary bits there for a front page, including a way for surfers to get to all other pages using hyperlinks, and a means for them to e-mail you.

Produce all your pages in the same way, adding then to FrontPage.

How to edit photographs

The only other computer skills that you need to acquire is in manipulating photos. There are various ways to get photos onto your PC's hard disk.

The same photograph with variations using Image Composer ▼ ▼

 Scan it in via a scanner. Obviously the image can come from a photograph, magazine, brochure or wherever else you can find it.

▷ Input directly a photo you have taken via a digital camera.

▷ Get a photo off the Internet (beware of copyright infringements) by downloading it onto your own hard disk.

Older versions of FrontPage come complete with an image editor called *Image Composer*. To find it, go into FrontPage Explorer, open the **Tools** menu and select **Show Image Editor**. If you do not have this, there are other good picture editors. You might like to try Microsoft's Image Editor (free with Windows 98) or Photo Editor (in the full Office 2000 suite), or Adobe PhotoShop (excellent, but not cheap) or PaintShop Pro (superb shareware from **www.jasc.com**).

Picture editors enable you to do all sorts of things with photos. The most important tools that you will actually use are comparatively easy to grasp, and will enable you to:

▷ change the size of the photograph

▷ cut out in irregular shape from a photograph

▷ crop a photograph.

The ability to juggle images is very important with Web sites, as the Internet is a photo-heavy medium – your site will need very many illustrations, and you need to vary your presentation.

Reduce the download time of your Web site, to make it friendly to visitors. Crunch your images to make sure the front page downloads in under 30 seconds (covered in Chapter 6).

The screen opposite shows how one photograph can be used in several different ways.

Picture editors enable you to do all sorts of things with photos

Remember to maximise the design for search engine prominence – check that your site is search engine friendly against your chosen keywords (see Chapter 6).

4: Publish and be damned

▼
▼
▼
▼
▼

Use FrontPage to publish you works for the world to read

Once you are happy with your results, you can use FrontPage to publish you works for the world to read. Make sure you have the address of your Web space at hand, then hit the **Publish** button on FrontPage Explorer's top toolbar. It will guide you through what to do.

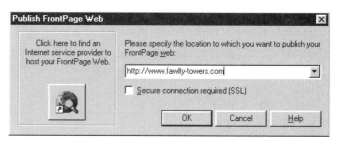

That connects you to the cyberspace you have reserved for yourself. And after you enter your password, your site will load automatically.

You are now on-line, and waiting for the first visitor to your Web site. Publishing is (or should be) as simple as that.

Costs

The cost of publishing a Web site yourself obviously depends on which option you select at each point in the decision-making process.

The figures given here are typical costs at the time of writing, mid-2000.

Name registration

This can be anything from nothing (i.e. using a sub-domain of your supplier, such as **www.virginbiz.com/ritzhotel**) to £10 if you can register it yourself, to up to £100 if a firm does it for you.

Having your own URL like **Corisande.com** or **rowhillgrange.co.uk** is better for a number of reasons – search engines give you more prominence and visitors see you as more 'professional'.

Web space

That is where your site 'lives' so that people can find it. This will be on a server that is permanently connected to the Internet.

It can cost you nothing (lots of companies offer free space), but there is usually a catch. Adverts may pop up, you may have to pay through the nose for any technical support or advice of any sort, or the server may be slow. In any event you have no recourse if the server is consistently unreliable.

At most you may pay around £200 a year for purchasing space on a commercial server. This should give you reliable service and as much technical support as you need.

Software

FrontPage plus picture editing software will cost between £150 and £300, depending upon the graphics package.

You can do it for nothing by utilising Notepad and a free File Transfer program, but don't consider this unless you have a lot of spare time – and perhaps a technically-proficient 14-year-old in the house.

▼
▼
▼
▼
▼

My own recommendation would be to use FrontPage and PaintShop Pro, register a domain and buy commercial cyberspace.

The total cost would be around £450 plus time to learn how to handle the software and carry out effective Web marketing. Obviously, if you cost out your time, it could put the total considerably higher.

Conclusion

This chapter has shown you how you can write a Web site using Front Page and publish it to a remote server.

To write your new Web site you would go through the following stages:

1　Lay out your ideas on design on paper.

2　The transfer to Web format using FrontPage software.

3　Add images and photos.

4　Compress photos to enable pages to load quicker.

5　Optimise the use of desired keywords, e.g. 'Cornwall hotels', for search engine recognition.

6　Register you desired name, e.g. 'www.corisande.com'.

7　Buy your cyberspace or sign up for free space.

8　Use FrontPage to publish your new site to your piece of cyberspace.

9　Register the site with search engines.

10　Regularly monitor the progress on search engines and make necessary changes.

9

Professional Web site design

If you cannot face learning the whole process of designing you own Web site, submitting it to search engines and maximising your search engine positioning against keywords, then you will need to get a professional to do the job for you.

For a very modest sum, a hotel can be featured on the AA or BTA site. Or you can pay anything from perhaps under £100 for a simple but adequate site on a travel specialist like Smooth Hound or Milford, to a £1000 for a larger site with a designer like Soft Options, to £2500 with company like Express Media and on up to several thousands if you want an all-singing, all-dancing multimedia site with a Web camera and other bolt-on extras. (All figures are approximate, and based on 2000 costs.)

Unfortunately not all Web sites are equal, nor do you necessarily get what you pay for. Let us try to guide you through the maze of options.

A sub-site of a big organisation

Really there are only two big 'official' sites to consider:

> The *AA* at **www.theaa.co.uk**

> The *British Tourist Authority* on **www.visitbritain.com**

The good news is that both these organisations get thousands of people a day looking at their sites. The bad news is that there are thousands of places offering accommodation on their databases.

From the point of view of an individual hotel, the number of people per day looking at the AA or BTA site is not relevant. What is relevant is the number looking at the average hotel site on that main site.

To see what the problem is from the viewpoint of the surfers, consider what happens when they find the **AA site** – around 8000 surfers a day get to the 'Where to Stay, Where to Eat' area of the site, where they will find around 8000 hotels and bed & breakfasts listed.

There is no charge for AA members, but you have no influence on the design, and the copy is what the AA choose to write about you. You can pay if you want for a link to your own Web site, but you still cannot influence the copy that they put in about you.

My own research shows that unless your accommodation is in one of the straightforward honeypots like London or Bath or Oxford, then you are unlikely to get more than one to five people a month using the paid link to visit your own Web site.

Remember too that surfers are surrounded by the choice of your competitors on a site like this.

To illustrate the point of how difficult is it for the browser to get to an individual hotel, let us take the example of a surfer getting to the BTA site. They have about 7000 surfers a day getting to their front page.

The front page of the BTA site

The surfer arrives at **http://www.visitbritain.com/**

First thing that happens is that they cannot get any further into the site without answering 'where are you travelling from?' At this stage some of the visitors will bale out. Those that answer the question get to:

The main links page at the BTA site

Let us say the surfers are not diverted by the articles or the banner advert, but find the **Accommodation** button, among the 16 others. They then get taken to a page, from where, either the '**Search for Hotels, guest houses and b&b**', or the '**Explore Hotels**' links will take them to a search page. Here they have to input a town. This is fine if you want a hotel in, say, Bath. The search will give a list of about 25 hotels in and around Bath, with the highlighted 5 in yellow at the top, being hotels that have paid for enhanced entries.

The Accommodation page offers several routes to search pages where you can hunt for accommodation ▶▶▶

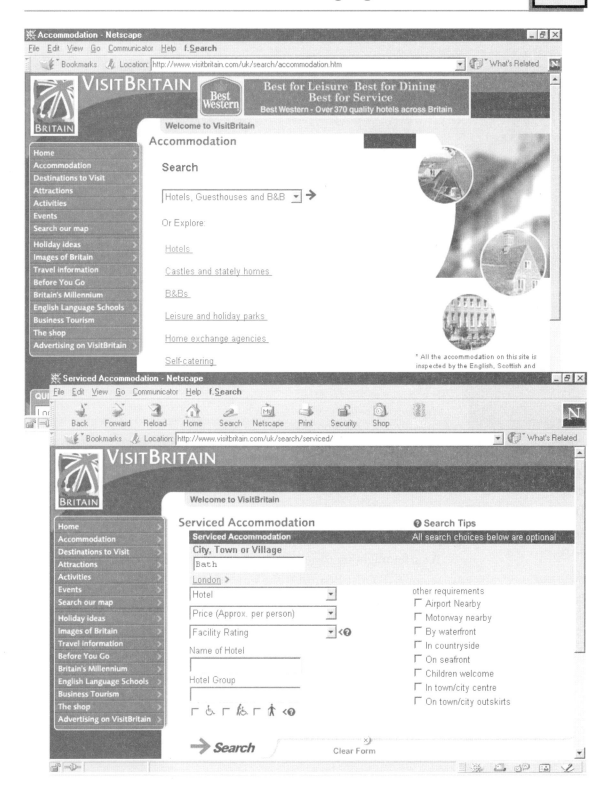

The results of a BTA
search for a hotel
in Bath

But if the surfer wants to stay in say Devon, then they have a problem, as the BTA only lets them select a *town*. As the chances are that the visitor has no idea where they want to stay, the rural hotel misses out, and it is really not worth their while being listed here.

A surfer might try to get some information on Devon via the link to the regional Tourist Board. At the time of writing, the links from the BTA to the regional tourist boards – around half of which have Web sites – were not working. Things may have improved by the time you read this.

To find your Web presence on a big site like the BTA, the visitor has to:

▷   know exactly which town they want to stay at, to have any chance of happening on your business;

▷   choose to get the details of your business from the 25 or so offered on that page.

The net result is that although the BTA claims to get around 7000 thousand visits per day with each visitor looking at 10 pages on average, they do have around 25,000 pages on their database, so few people find any one hotel.

My own experience is that a hotel can only expect a few referrals a year from a big site like this.

A sub-site of a travel specialist

Any business these days gets bombarded with advertising from commercial companies offering to put them on their site for a sum of money. How do you judge whether such companies can deliver any visitors to a Web page that you might purchase on their site?

The first thing would be to check them out on the Internet. Try their URL to see that it exists and look at what they have on their site. If it is just starting up, the best advice is to avoid it. Put yourself in the position of the Web user, not the hotel keeper. See whether you think the site is user friendly. Is it plastered in distracting adverts for other services (if so they are making money out of sending browsers to other sites)? Can you find information on it quickly and easily. If the site is not user friendly, then do not even think about using it.

Then go to a search engine and try to find whether their site is well positioned on search engines, using the kind of keywords that a browser would use. If you have a bed and breakfast in Wales, then use the query 'bed and breakfast in Wales' and see whether the people trying to sell you a Web site feature when that query is put in. If they themselves do not come up reasonably highly in search engine results on this test, then in all probability surfers will not find that site, and hence would not find your page on it if you were to buy one.

You will find that the majority of sites that advertise in this way are not worth spending money on. They are starting up, and for them to get any search engine positioning themselves these days will take at least six months. By search engine positioning I do not mean getting one listing,

Smooth Hound take
you straight into
their map-based
search system

I mean generating enough traffic through their site to bring individual establishments advertising there a reasonable number of enquirers.

There are only a few sites that have attracted traffic in any volume. The best known is Smooth Hound, who on a varying price scale will design and host a Web site for you within their site. This operates in a similar way to the AA. The front page gets straight to the point with a map of Britain.

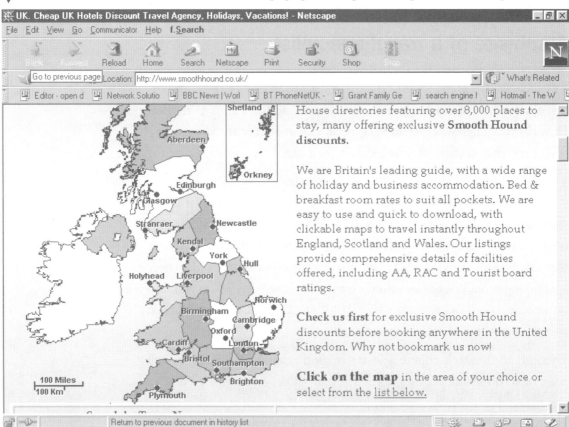

Click on the map, to, for example, find accommodation in the Yorkshire Dales, which gets us a map of Yorkshire, divided into areas. Clicking on the green area to get more on the Dales takes us to a close-up, with a list of towns. From these we try Leyburn at random, as we really have no idea where we want in the Dales, to get a list of places with brief details.

Select a town from the detailed maps, to get 'tombstone' abstracts of accommodation in the area   ▶▶▶

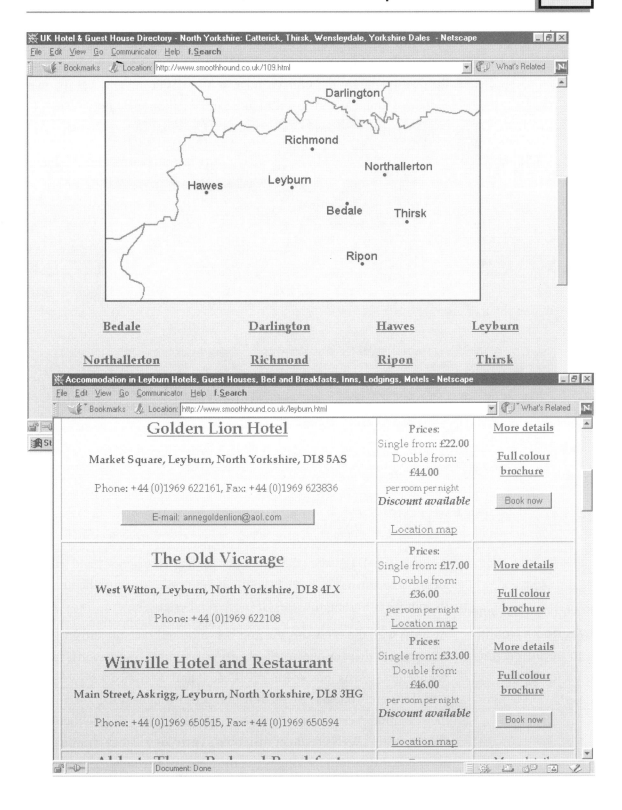

From the 16 'tombstone' abstracts of accommodation around Leyburn (arranged not unnaturally with the higher-paying sites at the top of the list), we might try the Old Vicarage at West Witton. This has its own Smooth Hound Web site with lots of information including prices.

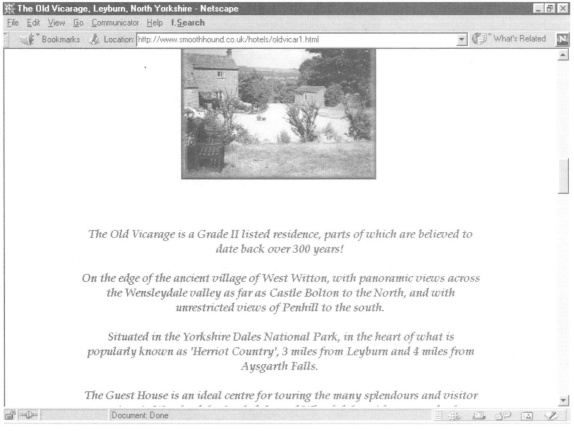

The Old Vicarage is a Grade II listed residence, parts of which are believed to date back over 300 years!

On the edge of the ancient village of West Witton, with panoramic views across the Wensleydale valley as far as Castle Bolton to the North, and with unrestricted views of Penhill to the south.

Situated in the Yorkshire Dales National Park, in the heart of what is popularly known as 'Herriot Country', 3 miles from Leyburn and 4 miles from Aysgarth Falls.

The Guest House is an ideal centre for touring the many splendours and visitor

These pages will have been designed by Smooth Hound and approved and paid for by the hotel.

As with the BTA site, the numbers finding 'honeypot', and clearly identifiable, towns like Bath, Edinburgh or London are much higher than the numbers finding the sites of more rural establishments.

Again as with the BTA site, the number of other hotels advertising their wares means that any one hotel's chances of getting a reservation is lower. With eight towns given for the Dales, and a choice of over 100 establishments, one has to ask 'how the surfer will make a choice?'. Will they examine every town, or choose a couple at random? Will they look at every hotel's Web site under that town's entry, or will they choose some at random? Random looking is the most likely outcome.

My own feeling is that outside of listings under London and a very few other towns, then the average number of visits to an individual hotel's Web page on Smooth Hound is in the region of one or two a day. In an environment that requires around 100 visits to actually get a booking, this means that you would get five to ten bookings a year from such a site.

On the other hand, you will have paid only around £50 for the advert. It is not volume booking, but it is value for money. Of the sites available, Smooth Hound is the only one that I have come across that I could honestly make this statement for. The other sites that I have looked at for my own hotel have been more hit or miss, delivering the odd reservation if one was lucky.

A Web site on a non-travel-specific site

There are any number of non-travel-specific sites on the Web like Scoot (www.scoot.co.uk) that will offer you the opportunity to park your details on their server. Scoot asks for a query and then attempts to answer that query from what it has on its database.

Virgin Biz (www.virginbiz.net) also enables you to build your own site on their server, with more or less support depending on how much you want to pay them. In the range £500 to £850 you get your own URL, Web space to put it in and telephone guidance to build your own site. For £500 you get to do it yourself with an on-line form, and they give you half an hour telephone support, plus submission with search engines (this will not guarantee you search engine placing, just that they will submit to a number of search engines for you).

A designed site, with your own URL

For this you will need to find a suitable Web design company. Once you have found them, either brief them or follow their advice to get the site designed, up and running. After that you would expect a search engine submission programme, and management of your site for a year.

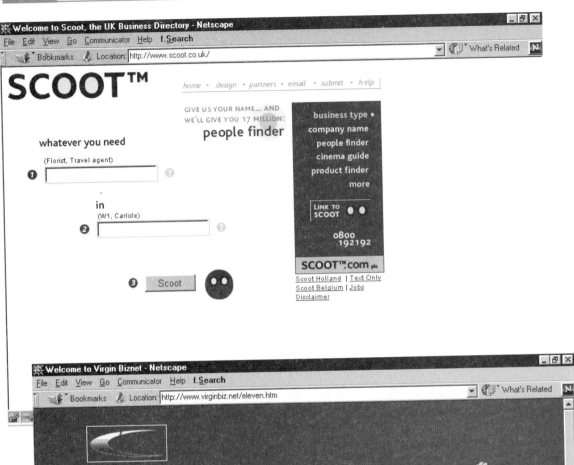

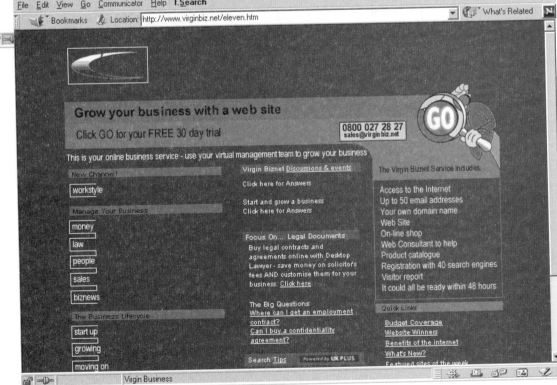

◄◄◄ Non-travel-specific host sites include Scoot (top)
and VirginBiz.net (below)

Management should include supplying you with Web site statistics, re-submission to search engines as appropriate and changes of a reasonable nature that you may require over the year (price changes, updated photographs and things of that nature).

First find your Web designer.

▷ Go to a search engine and interrogate it with keywords like 'Web design UK hotels', or look in the appropriate category at a directory like Yahoo, to get lists of designers.

▷ Go to a search engine and see what sites come up when you type in the keywords that you are interested in for your own business. Then look at those sites to see who designed them.

▷ Ask around owners of similar businesses or at industry gatherings to find who has a Web site with which they are happy.

Look at the Web designers' sites to see what you could expect to pay and what you would get for that money, then look again – and look at some of their clients' sites – to get an idea of the quality of their work.

There are a number of Web design companies that specialise in the hotel industry. Among them are the following (with prices as of mid-2000):

▷ *Soft Options* (www.soft-options.co.uk) – my own company – charges £950 for the design and maintenance of a Web site. Visit the site for details of what you get for that, who their clients are, plus information about search engines, Web statistics and so on.

▷ *Dedicate* (www.dedicate.co.uk) – based in the Lake District. Their site gives a cost of £600 for the Web space and registration of your URL. On top of that there is an unspecified amount for designing and maintaining your Web site, which will push the total cost well above £1,000.

▷ *Oxlink* (www.oxlink.co.uk) – covering mainly Oxfordshire. Oxlink will register your URL for £160 and go on from there to write and host your site. You could expect the total cost to be around £2,000.

▷ *Express Media* (www.expressmedia.co.uk) will design and host a 10 page site for £2500 or a 30 page site for £4650. The Gleneagles Hotel sites is an example of what you can expect for more money.

What happens once you choose a Web designer

Obviously you need to agree the cost, and size of the Web site, what you will supply in the way of photographs, illustrations and copy plus a clear understanding of what the designer will supply.

Many Web designers will only lay out the wording that you have sent them, they will not write it for you. Similarly there are likely to be restrictions on the number of photographs on the site, and the format that you supply them in. Some will only accept digital photographs.

You must also decide at this stage the keywords that you want the site to use for the search engines. For example, a site with the obvious keywords for a 'B&B in Bradford' is unlikely to be found by a surfer looking for a 'Yorkshire hotel'. If you want to be found against the latter, then you have to brief accordingly at this stage.

Keyword targets can only be very narrow – you cannot have your cake and eat it in the Web game. If you write a site against a wide variety of keywords, the site will end up doing badly against all of them.

You will also need to agree what to expect in the way of site management.

Search engines. Which will it be registered with? Remember that only a handful actually matter. Being submitted to 500 search engines is and unnecessary, as 490 of them could never deliver viable traffic, even if your site came high on its positioning.

Key word targets can only be very narrow

◀◀◀ Check out the designers' sites to get details of their packages (e.g. Soft Options, above), and look at some of their clients' sites (e.g. Gleneagles Hotels, by Express Media, below)

No Web designer can guarantee that you will appear on a particular search engine database (sometimes they will go several months without adding any sites at all). Nor can you be guaranteed good positioning, and even if you could then other keywords would give a different result.

Look instead at some of the Web sites that they have designed and try to find those sites using the sort of keywords that someone would use if they were looking for accommodation in that area. See if that Web designer's sites come high up on the search engine's listing.

Web site statistics. Make sure you get regular statistics from your supplier, detailing how many individual visitors come to your site. Make sure you are not palmed off with hits – remembering that a single visitor can generate many hits (see page 103 – 200 hits a day may sound impressive, but might represents only five or six people visiting the site.

If you do not understand the figures that you get from your supplier, then carry on asking for clarification until you do.

First you have to get the surfers to look at your site, rather than at one of the others out there, then convert the visit into a sale. Obviously you will not convert them all, as a fair number are probably 'browsing' without intending to 'buy'. Remember you need about 100 visits to make a sale.

Maintenance. Make sure you know how often you can change copy or photographs. For example, change prices, put on new picture of the garden in summer, or a menu in the restaurant. Once you have had a site up and running for a while, you may well find that you need to add pages or alter it. Check in advance that your designer will do this for you. But note that no designer will completely re-design your site every few months without charging you more.

Conclusion

A good professionally-written site will probably bring you many more visits than writing one yourself. Having said that you could do just as well as the professionals if you were prepared to learn to write and publish your own site, and then to learn to market it using search engine submissions and linking to other sites.

Some of the most visited hotel sites on the Web are written and maintained by amateurs who have done it themselves. But they have spent a considerable amount of their own time doing it, and get some sort of personal pleasure out of the experience.

In other words, you have to like playing with computers, and be prepared to invest a considerable amount of time, before you even consider taking the Do It Yourself route.

The balance is in the time required to learn to do it properly yourself. The Internet is littered with poorly written sites that people have done themselves and which are found by surfers only by accident. The purpose of this book is not to 'name and shame' such sites, just to observe that there are many of them out there.

The cost of a poor site that nobody finds, is a substantial lost opportunity cost. You may well stand to gain around 10% on your turnover by having a good Web site, but as the Web becomes more the norm in society, then it will mean that you will start to lose turnover unless you have a good site.

For most businesses, a good professional designer will build and maintain a site that will bring you more visits but will cost you more than doing it yourself.

The choice is yours, but by now you should understand how to acquire a Web site either by publishing it yourself or getting assistance, and how to market it in the real or in the abstract. But whatever route you take, you should now know what questions to ask, and how to judge the answers.

As we progress into the 21st century, then you will have to get your business onto the Internet in one way or another. You can get by with learning to use e-mail and having a small presence on a large site. However it is unlikely that this will be enough, and sooner or later you will have to have your own site. The sooner you do this, the more you will get out of 'dot com' in the long term.

Index